Things That BITE

A REALISTIC LOOK AT CRITTERS THAT SCARE PEOPLE

by Tom Anderson

ADVENTURE PUBLICATIONS, INC.
CAMBRIDGE, MINNESOTA

To Nancy, for your love, support and love bites.

Acknowledgments

Grateful acknowledgments to the many who directly or indirectly made this book possible.

In the summer of 1993, I was paddling on the upper reaches of the Seal River in northern Manitoba on a Science Museum of Minnesota trip with guide and dear friend Cliff Jacobson. The bugs were bad and I jokingly suggested that Cliff write a book on the Basic Essentials of Things That Bite. He waved the mosquitoes from his face, looked at me and said, "No, Tom, that is a book you should write." Since that summer, not a year has passed when Cliff hasn't asked me about the book's progress. So thanks, Cliff, for your urgings, support and confidence. I am hoping we can share more campfires in places where things bite.

This book would not have been possible without the input and suggested species to include from the many frontline naturalists, teachers and biologists across the country, particularly in the Southwest, who interface on a regular basis with people in the outdoors. Too numerous to name, you know who you are.

Abundant thanks go to Dr. David Richman, arachnid expert and curator of the Arthropod Museum at New Mexico State University, the skilled Arizona field herpetologist, Bryan D. Hughes, mosquito expert Mike Riehle from the University of Arizona, and herpetologist extraordinaire, John Moriarty.

Thanks to Gerri and Gordon Slabaugh of Adventure Publications for having faith in me and for really paying attention to my suggestions. That means a lot. Monica Ahlman and Brett Ortler at Adventure also made this project fun and easy to work on.

A day doesn't pass when I don't feel such gratitude to being married to the best editor, supporter, business partner, coach and playmate in the whole world! Thanks, Nancy, you are such a gift to me.

Finally, this book would not have been possible if there had not been a wonderful host of critters that love the taste of me. Imagine a world without "things that bite"! Wait . . . without them we would likely be dead. Hail the complex web of biological diversity!

Edited by Brett Ortler

Cover and book design by Jonathan Norberg
Cartoon illustrations by Erik Ahlman and Brenna Slabaugh
All chapter introduction artwork by Julie Martinez

See page 167 for photo credits by photographer and page number.

Things That
BITE

Table of Contents

Aware, Not Afraid

The last word in ignorance is the man who says of an animal or plant:
"What good is it?" If the land mechanism as a whole is good, then every part is
good, whether we understand it or not. If the biota, in the course of eons, has
built something we like but do not understand, then who but a fool would discard
seemingly useless parts? To keep every cog and wheel is the first precaution of
intelligent tinkering.   —Aldo Leopold

Our nature, as humans, is to play favorites. Things that inflict pain tend to be "bad." Conversely, those species that we depend on for food or that provide us with recreational opportunities (such as hunting and fishing) are labeled as "good." We are categorical by nature. Humans are the only species that judge the "goodness" or "badness" of other creatures.

I want to challenge the reader to marvel in the adaptations of the biters and stingers in this book. Each has a unique set of adaptations, genius in design and function, and each plays an important role that benefits the whole system—including us. We should stand in wonder and awe of these beasts, and in so doing, come to know them and their places better.

The more we learn about something, the more we understand and respect it. It is doubtful that if you kill any of the stingers and biters in this book, you will significantly impact their population. However, remember you have a choice, and that they are not biting because they are "bad."

Each of us harbors fears. Research verifies that children learn many of their fears from adults, particularly their parents. A toddler who watches his parents cringe or overreact when a wasp flies near him, or when a spider or snake suddenly appears, will learn that such a response is normal. Children are not used to seeing their parents cringe in fear. This becomes an emotional bookmark in the child's life and is not easily forgotten. One of the best gifts you can give your child is to demonstrate curiosity and enthusiasm about the oddities (and yes, even the outcasts) of the animal world. This is a perfect opportunity to teach children respect, not fear.

It is important to note that a few critters bite or sting as part of their strategy for obtaining food, but many species will bite or sting only if they feel threatened or are mishandled. For many of the creatures covered in this book, the customary way to deal with them is to quickly kill them. Besides the obvious ethical issues involved with this approach, some of the critters in this book (such as the Gila monster) are illegal to kill. Others, such as javelinas and bears, have seasons regulating when they can be harvested.

It is my hope that the reader will look past the potentially troublesome aspects of these creatures and recognize how beneficial these biters and stingers are. Not only will I introduce the reader to the basic natural history of the animal, but I will give advice on how to avoid conflicts, and if necessary, how to treat a bite or sting.

This book is intended as a guide to animal species that might make an outing uncomfortable or painful, and can accompany a trip to a state park, a picnic, a day on the trout stream, camping, canoeing or backpacking. It can make your fishing expedition, backyard picnic or party more comfortable.

I used my judgment to determine which species to include in this book. As a naturalist, I am an educator and nature is often my classroom. I have had the good fortune of leading groups on various eco-trips throughout North America and into South America. Each area has its own unique assemblage of creatures. This book deals with species found in the Southwest. Specifically, I have attempted to address the fauna found in southern New Mexico, Arizona, southern Utah, Nevada and southern California.

In the United States, the Southwest covers the southwestern corner of the Lower 48 states. While it is often perceived to be a vast arid wasteland, it is very biologically diverse and encompasses an expansive range of ecosystems, including everything from deserts to forested mountains. These habitats host a variety of wildlife, too many species to include in this book. So I owe a special thanks to the naturalists, federal and state park personnel and outdoor recreationists who provided me with lists of critters that most commonly bother or concern them and—more importantly—the public, at their respective centers or parks. This book, and particularly the list of biters and stingers, would not have been possible without their input.

While I respect that many people are wary of many species in this book, I can assure you that it is highly unlikely that you will ever be injured by a wolf, a bear, a cougar, a coyote, a skunk, or a bat. Such species were added to this guide primarily to dispel myths and unfounded fears about them.

yellow jacket

Contrary to popular belief, the most deadly creatures in the United States are insects such as bees, and wasps. Approximately 50 people die each year in the U.S. from allergic reactions to bee, wasp or hornet stings, while an average of 15 people die from venomous snake bites, and an average of only 1 person a year dies from an attack of a large wild mammal.

To put things in perspective, I visited with an emergency room physician to ask about animal bites and stings. I asked, "Of all the bites and stings you deal with, which give you the greatest concern?" Almost immediately he responded, "Humans."

"Certainly, " he added, "we sometimes have to deal with disfiguring dog bites, but the ones that invariably lead to nasty infections are those delivered by humans." It turns out that legions of nasty anaerobic bacteria thrive between our teeth. Each of us can tolerate our own community of bacteria but not someone else's.

Of all the four-legged beasts in the Southwest and the wider United States, dogs, man's "best friend," are responsible for many, many more bites (and deaths) than any wild animal. According to the Arizona Department of Vital Statistics, over the period of 1999–2009, 16 people died as a result of dog-inflicted injuries. In 2010 alone, 34 human deaths were caused by dog bites in the United States, and more than 1,000 patients were admitted daily to U.S. emergency rooms because of dog bites.

Over that same decade, just under 1,000 people died from drowning in Arizona. Many of those victims were likely swimmers and swimming is considered a healthy pastime, not a dangerous one. The 934 drownings far surpassed the 4 deaths from venomous snake bites.

Another reality check is the fact that humans attack and kill their own fellow humans at a rate over 90,000 times the rate that bears attack us.

My hope is that this book will encourage you to explore the outdoors armed with a little more knowledge and with tips to make your experience more comfortable and pleasant. To get a better appreciation of the natural world and its role in our lives, we absolutely need the intimate connection of getting out there.

Enjoy the outdoors, and be aware—not afraid!

— Tom

Anaphylactic Shock, Rabies and a Dose of Reality

The majority of the time, most pain you will feel from a bite or a sting will likely be temporary. The likelihood of being bitten by a rabid mammal or experiencing a severe allergic reaction to a sting is small. However, you need to be observant and aware of the biter/stinger. The following information is intended to educate the reader about anaphylactic shock and rabies.

Anaphylaxis is a serious allergic reaction resulting from an insect sting, a bug bite or from exposure to food or drug allergens. Anaphylactic shock is the condition that can result from anaphylaxis, if left untreated. Rabies is a life-threatening virus that attacks the central nervous system.

Having some background and knowledge of these two uncommon afflictions will make your outdoor experience more comfortable. The irony is that it's more likely that you'll be injured when traveling by automobile than come down with either rabies or anaphylactic shock. Keep things in perspective.

ANAPHYLAXIS
Development of the following signs and symptoms within minutes of exposure to a bite or sting is a strong indication of anaphylaxis:

- Constriction of the airways that results in difficulty breathing
- Shock associated with a severe decrease in blood pressure
- Weak and rapid pulse
- Confusion or anxiety
- Dizziness or fainting
- Hives and itching
- Flushed or pale skin
- Nausea, vomiting or diarrhea

If you've had anaphylaxis or have a history of allergies or asthma, you may have a greater chance of having an anaphylactic reaction. Ask your doctor about obtaining an Anaphylaxis Emergency Treatment Kit or an EpiPen. Both contain injectable adrenaline (epinephrine) for allergic reactions.

RABIES

Rabies is a viral disease that invades the central nervous system of mammals, including humans. The virus is commonly transmitted in saliva, when an infected animal bites another animal or a person.

- The origin of the word "rabies" comes from the Latin word *rabere,* which means "to rave or rage."

- Globally, more than 55,000 people die of rabies each year. Dogs are responsible for 99 percent of those deaths. Fortunately, few rabies deaths occur in the United States due to successful pet vaccination efforts.

- In the Southwest, rabies is most commonly found in bats, followed by skunks. It also shows up in other mammals such as foxes, raccoons, coyotes, bobcats, cougars, javelinas, and domestic cats and dogs. There have even been isolated cases in livestock.

- Most recent cases of rabies in humans in the United States have occurred after the victim was bitten by an infected bat. (Reality check: It is estimated that less than 1 percent of bats carry rabies.) However, bats are rarely the cause of a rabies outbreak. They generally transmit the virus to other bats.

- In most areas where rabies outbreaks occur, the virus strain is traced back to dogs, cats, raccoons, skunks or other animals.

- After receiving an infectious bite, it takes 20–60 days for the virus to reach your brain. Early symptoms might be subtle. These could include headache, sore throat, fatigue or fever.

- Treatment for rabies is no longer the horror story we used to hear about. You know, multiple shots in your belly. You will initially receive a shot of human rabies immune globulin (HRIG) near the site of the bite. The following series of 5 vaccination shots will be in the upper arm.

- If you are bitten by an animal and are unable to have the biting animal tested for rabies, you absolutely need to receive the rabies shots.

- Untreated, the rabies virus is fatal 100 percent of the time!

- The best prevention is to not handle or touch wild mammals. Don't be tempted to help a sick-looking animal. Seek out help from properly trained wildlife professionals.

No-see-ums

Despite their small size, these little gnats can drive people crazy and to the nearest shelter. I have known folks to pack up their tents, hook up their trailers and leave spectacular campgrounds to avoid a major hatch of no-see-ums.

No-see-ums can inflict misery simply due to their sheer numbers. Sometimes swarms are so thick that they are easily taken into our mouths, nose, ears and eyes.

About No-see-ums

These little insects fall into a group known as biting midges, punkies and no-see-ums. There are over 100 species in North America. When these little flying insurgents are bad, they can be worse than mosquitoes since they can easily infiltrate the average window screen.

Life and Times . . .

Like other flies, these tiny biters go through a complete metamorphosis. They go from egg to larva to pupa before finally reaching adulthood. This metamorphosis can take 2–6 weeks.

After ingesting a blood meal, the female seeks the edge of a wetland, where she lays her eggs on moist soil or mud. Some species can produce up to 450 eggs per batch. Eggs generally hatch within 2–10 days. The adult female only lives a few weeks.

The tiny aquatic and legless larvae scavenge in mud, sand, tree holes, water and vegetation. Species found in the Southwest spend the winter in a dormant state in their larval stage and pupate in the spring, and emerge as adults.

Males usually emerge first and are ready to mate when the females take wing. Mating usually occurs in flight, when receptive females fly into swarms of cooperative males.

Fascinating Facts

- No-see-ums belong to the order of true flies or *Diptera*, which translates to "two wings." There are more than 3,500 Diptera species in North America.

- While there are currently no issues with no-see-ums transmitting diseases to humans in the Southwest, they are blamed for spreading bluetongue (a serious disease in ruminants such as sheep and cattle) among livestock in parts of the United States.

Thanks to No-see-ums

- No-see-ums are very important in the food chain, as many species of insects and fish feed on the larvae, pupae and adult insects.

- These tiny insects, particularly the nectar-seeking males, are important plant pollinators.

Myth Busters

MYTH: The female no-see-um dies after 1 egg-laying episode.

While this is true for some species, some females lay a second batch of eggs.

Why They Bite

Male no-see-ums do not bite. But the female needs a protein-rich blood meal in order to produce her eggs. She obtains it by biting a variety of involuntary donors such as reptiles, amphibians, birds and mammals—including humans.

Remarkably, some species of no-see-ums prey upon other insects, ingesting hemolymph, the equivalent of insect blood.

How They Bite

Like other biting flies, the female no-see-um has a tiny set of sharp mandibles, or jaws, that are used to cut into flesh. A natural blood thinner in her saliva makes it easier for her to suck up blood and helps to quickly secure a meal.

In itself, the nonvenomous bite is not exceedingly painful. However, after the injury has been dealt, the itching and discomfort can be miserable.

How Afraid Should I Be?

Other than temporary discomfort, there is little reason to worry. Small raised red welts and blisters can form and last for several days. The greatest concern is that sometimes an allergic reaction can occur. Such a reaction will usually show up resembling a skin rash or infection.

Preventing No-see-um Bites

- The simplest protection to prevent bites is to wear protective clothing (long pants and long-sleeved shirts).

- Insect repellents containing DEET (N, N-diethyl-meta-toluamide) help reduce the likelihood of bites.

- Since their small size allows them to crawl through the conventional 16-mesh wire window screen, a finer mesh might be required to keep them outdoors.

- These tiny flies are weak fliers, so indoor fans at high speeds can be used to keep the insects out of small areas.

- Some people have good luck with a spray-on sunscreen (SPF 30). Although it is DEET-free, it is recommended that you shower it off each night.

THINK TWICE

Think twice about where you want to hike, picnic or camp. No-see-ums tend to stay in the vicinity of their wetland breeding grounds. Avoid these areas, particularly at dawn and dusk, when these insects are most active.

Think twice about leaving your porch light on. No-see-ums are attracted to lights.

Treatment of Bites

- Clean the bites with soap and water.

- Itching and swelling can be reduced with the help of anti-itch and anti-inflammatory lotions and creams.

- Aspirin or Tylenol might offer additional relief. Do not administer aspirin to children under 15 years old.

- If blisters occur, apply an antibacterial/antibiotic ointment and keep the blisters loosely covered to allow air passage to help dry them out.

BOTTOM LINE

Protective clothing and other simple precautions will keep most no-see-ums at bay. But other than a little temporary discomfort, there is no reason to fear them. Their bite is neither venomous nor very painful. And although the itching and welts can be miserable, the discomfort is typically short-lived.

Chiggers

There is something so inviting about pausing along the lush grassy edge of a stream, a pond or a lake. These are popular places to picnic, nap or sunbathe, but such episodes of relaxation can turn miserable if there are chiggers lurking nearby. Unbeknownst to you, these tiny, stealthy mites can make their way onto your body where they delicately probe your skin. As their bite is imperceptible, you will likely learn that chiggers were present in the area after the fact—when you go to bed and the itching begins. Woe to the person who begins scratching! It only makes it worse.

About Chiggers

Like ticks and spiders, chiggers are arachnids, not insects. Chiggers start out very small; their larvae are only $1/150$ of an inch in diameter, and it's actually these tiny larvae that cause us discomfort.

As chiggers develop, they grow larger and their diet changes. As nymphs and adults, chiggers no longer feed upon us; they prey upon insect eggs and small invertebrates in the soil.

While not especially common in the Southwest, chiggers are found primarily in river valleys.

Life and Times . . .

Like other arachnids, chiggers go through 4 life stages: egg, larva, nymph and adult. The complete life cycle takes roughly 50–70 days.

Adult male chiggers die shortly after mating. Fertilized females lay up to 400 eggs in early spring after the soil begins to warm. The female chigger dies shortly after laying her eggs.

In a matter of days, the eggs hatch, producing the chigger's tiny larval stage, which is barely visible to the naked eye. Shortly after hatching, the six-legged larvae climb to a perch, where they can easily latch onto a passing host. Unlike their tick cousins, which sit and wait, chigger larvae are nearly constantly on the move. Larvae feed on a number of host species, including mammals, birds, reptiles and even some amphibians.

Larvae are most likely to be found in areas with thick vegetation and high humidity. Due to the arid environment of the Southwest, river valleys often provide the best chigger habitat. Due to their thin skin and small size, these unusual animals are susceptible to dehydration. Sandy, dry areas are not humid enough for their survival.

After 3 days of feeding on the host, the larva drops off and crawls into the soil where it develops into the nymph stage. Nymphs are essentially scaled-down versions of adults and feed on tiny soil invertebrates until they are ready to change into adults. Both nymphs and adults have 8 legs.

Three generations of chiggers are born over the course of spring, summer and early fall.

Fascinating Facts

- A larval chigger's saliva includes an enzyme that turns skin cells into a liquid, which the larva then drinks.

- Like mosquitoes, chiggers are attracted to the carbon dioxide given off by a passing host.

- Chiggers are capable of getting all over a person's body in minutes. The climb from a victim's shoe to the belt line (a favorite point of attack) is an ascent that takes about 15 minutes. That's no small feat for such a small creature; when climbing on a human host, a chigger covers a distance equal to 5,000 times its total length. That's akin to a human climbing a tall mountain on an empty stomach!

Thanks to Chiggers

- A chigger's favorite foods include eggs of springtails (tiny soil insects), isopods (terrestrial crustaceans such as wood lice) and even pesky mosquitoes!

- Chiggers, like other parasites, are a sign of a healthy and diverse natural world.

Myth Busters

MYTH: Itching is caused by chiggers that burrow under your skin and die.

Chiggers never burrow under skin, and they don't die on their host. Only their delicate mouthparts pierce the skin; the small dot visible inside the welt is called the *stylostome* and is the tube where the chigger feeds. The female jigger, or chigoe flea, does literally attach by burrowing under skin to lay its eggs.

MYTH: Chiggers get their red color from feeding on blood.

Actually, chiggers are born red. Chiggers feed on liquefied skin tissue, not blood. After a full meal, a chigger turns yellow.

MYTH: Nail polish applied to chigger welts helps relieve the itch.

This myth persists because of the belief that the nail polish will smother the chigger, preventing it from inflicting more pain. Nevertheless, the stylostome, not the chigger, causes the itching. If there's a welt, it's probably too late; the chigger has fed and is long gone.

Why They Bite

Remember, chiggers only bite as youngsters, during their larval stage of development. In order to develop properly they must feed on the skin tissue of a host. Later in life, they feed on insects and vegetation in the soil.

How They Bite

Like ticks, chiggers insert microscopic beak-like mouthparts into skin depressions in the host. These piercing mouthparts are delicate and can only penetrate thin skin, such as skin follicles, or areas where skin wrinkles and folds. That's why most chigger bites occur around the ankles, the armpits, the back of the knees and below the belt line.

At least 1 hour, and more likely 2–3 hours, pass before the chigger actually starts feeding. The chigger releases enzymes that liquefy the skin, and the body reacts by hardening the cells on all sides of the saliva route. Eventually a hard tubelike structure called a *stylostome* is formed.

> **THINK TWICE**
>
> Think twice about sitting down for a rest or picnic in thick grassy or brushy areas.
>
> Think twice about aggressively scratching any chigger bites. Your scratching can lead to a secondary infection.

This pipelike structure contains the digesting saliva; the chigger inserts its delicate mouthparts into the stylostome and sucks up the liquid skin tissue. In this way, the stylostome serves as something like a tall drinking glass.

If a chigger feeds undisturbed, the stylostome and surrounding tissue become inflamed, creating an itchy red welt. The longer the chigger feeds, the deeper the stylostome grows, and the larger the welt becomes.

If undisturbed, the chigger remains on the host for 3–4 days. Though you might detect the first bites in a matter of 3–4 hours, the worst itching generally occurs 24–48 hours after the first bites.

How Afraid Should I Be?

There is no need to be overly afraid of chigger bites. Though the itching can be agonizing and persistent for a couple of days, chigger bites don't cause any human diseases or long-term disabilities. With that said, try not to scratch chigger bites; vigorous scratching can lead to secondary infections.

Preventing Chigger Bites

- Avoiding chiggers is the best prevention, so it's important to choose the right clothing for your outings in chigger country. Lightly colored, tightly knit clothing offers better protection from wandering chiggers and keeps you cooler. Tightly woven socks, long sleeves and long pants are a good choice, and it's best to tuck your pants into your boots or shoes. Be sure to button collars to close off additional access points. *Do not* wear shorts, sleeveless shirts, sandals or any clothing that gives chiggers easy access to your skin.

- Mosquito repellents can help prevent chigger bites. Apply repellent to exposed skin and around openings in clothes, such as cuffs, waistbands, shirtfronts and boot tops, as this forces chiggers to cross the treated line to get inside your clothes. It's important to apply repellent often, as it only remains potent for short periods.

- Powdered sulfur, which is also known as sublimed sulfur, is an excellent deterrent against chiggers when applied around openings in clothing. It is available at most pharmacies. If you are in a heavily infested area, rub the powdered sulfur over the skin on your arms, legs and waist. Some outdoor enthusiasts rub on a mixture of half talcum powder and half sulfur powder. Before using powdered sulfur, be aware that sulfur has a strong, rotten egg-like odor, and it is a skin irritant for some people. Experiment on a small skin area the first time you try it.

- While outside, avoid tall grasses and brush. If you're going to sit down on something, choose a rock that has been heated by the sun. Chiggers avoid objects that are hotter than 99 °F. (Temperatures below 42 °F will kill them.)

- After an outing outdoors, change clothes as soon as possible, and wash them before wearing them again. If you don't, the chiggers will simply get to you next time you put them on.

- To avoid encounters closer to home and keep chiggers out of your yard, remove their preferred habitat by clearing brush and weeds. Chiggers don't do well in areas that are well groomed.

Treatment of Bites

- The best treatment for chigger bites is a warm and soapy bath. Vigorous scrubbing will remove any attached and feeding chiggers before the itching begins. If bathing is not an option, chiggers can be removed by thoroughly rubbing bare skin down with a towel or cloth.

- If chigger bites develop, itching can persist for 2 weeks. Over-the-counter local anesthetic creams such as benzocaine and camphor-phenol can provide some relief. Other treatment options include topical corticosteroids, oral antihistamines, and soothing compresses such as Domeboro or Aveeno. Rarely, some people are allergic to chigger bites and require prescription medications.

- Some home remedies are popular; many people swear that itching subsides if you apply a paste of meat tenderizer (salt-free papain) or baking soda on the welts. Another popular home remedy for itching relief is to sponge vinegar on welts.

- Some home remedies for chigger bites involve household chemicals. These "treatments" often include dangerous chemicals such as kerosene, turpentine, ammonia, alcohol, gasoline, salt or dry-cleaning fluid. Such chemicals can be harmful and the treatments don't work, so don't try them.

- Don't scratch chigger bites too vigorously, as this can lead to a nasty secondary bacterial infection. If you do scratch, disinfect the chigger bite with topical antiseptics.

- Eventually your body will break down the cause of your itch—the feeding tube of the chigger. Patience is a good virtue in dealing with chigger bites.

BOTTOM LINE

You can avoid chigger bites by wearing the proper clothing, watching where you sit or walk, and by taking precautions after venturing outdoors. If you develop welts from chigger bites, you can find comfort in knowing that the itching will be gone in a couple of weeks.

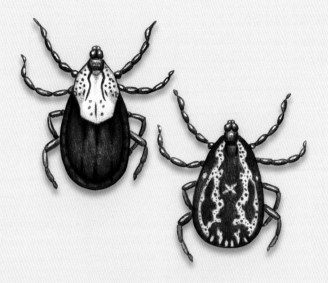

Ticks

Casually ask someone, "Is that a tick on your arm?" and you will likely witness an immediate and urgent response. For such a little fellow—no bigger than one of these typed letters—the tick easily prompts even the most macho of men to take defensive action. And even after the hitchhiking tick is pointed out, there is the predictable, contagious outbreak of twitching and scratching among people nearby.

Such is the power of this little creature.

(above left: female dog or wood tick; above right: male dog or wood tick)

About Ticks

Ticks are not insects. Like spiders, mites and scorpions, they are arachnids. Adult ticks have 8 legs, while the larvae have 6 legs.

dog or wood tick   black-legged or deer tick   Rocky Mountain wood tick

Thankfully, ticks are not a major pest in the Southwest. There are roughly 25–30 species found here with the most common being the brown dog tick.

The Rocky Mountain wood tick is about ⅛ of an inch in length and slightly larger after it ingests a blood meal. These brown ticks turn gray when engorged. The female has a gray-colored disk behind her head, while the male's disk is mottled brown and gray.

Like the Rocky Mountain wood tick, the American dog tick is also referred to as a wood tick; it is the larger of the two, approximately ¼ inch in length. The female has a cream-colored disk behind her head, while the male lacks the disk and has 2 thin, lighter-colored stripes running down his back. This tick is the primary carrier of Rocky Mountain spotted fever.

Unlike wood ticks, black-legged ticks have no white or cream-colored markings on their backs. They are smaller (about ⅛ inch long), dark brown to black and teardrop shaped. Females usually have an area behind their head that is orange to red in color. Black-legged ticks are the primary transmitter of Lyme disease.

Life and Times . . .

Under ideal conditions, ticks have a 2-year life cycle that includes blood-feeding stages as larvae, nymphs and adults. In the spring, tick eggs hatch and tiny larval ticks emerge. Sometimes referred to as seed ticks, they typically feed on the blood of small rodents such as mice. After developing into nymphs, they feed on small- to medium-sized mammals such as chipmunks. Adults seek out larger animals, including white-tailed deer. Because female black-legged ticks secure blood meals from deer for egg production, deer play a key role in maintaining high tick populations.

In the Southwest, humans are most at risk from May to September when the tick is in the nymph stage. However, adult ticks can bite, so caution is advised from April through December.

Fascinating Facts

- Ticks have been reported to feed on at least 125 different kinds of animals, including 57 bird varieties, 54 mammal species, and 14 types of lizards.

- The folds in a tick's skin allow it to greatly expand in size. An engorged female tick might increase her weight by 200 times!

Thanks to Ticks

- Ticks are prey for many species of birds and an important part of the food chain.

Myth Busters

MYTH: Ticks will leap out of trees onto you!

Ticks are crawlers, not jumpers. Leaping insects, such as crickets or grasshoppers, have longer, larger legs. A tick's legs are better suited for climbing up to ambush sites where they stretch out their front legs, as if signaling a touchdown. This posture is referred to as questing. Ticks will sit on grass stems or twigs for hours questing, waiting to attach to a passing host.

Why They Bite

Simply put, ticks bite only to secure a meal. They require blood meals to change from one life stage to the next. An adult female also requires a blood meal to produce her thousands of eggs.

How They Bite

An electron microscope image of a tick's mouthparts is reminiscent of the aliens portrayed in the *Star Wars* movies. Creepy!

The tick's beak-like mouthparts have backward-pointing barbs that allow the tick to remain anchored for a successful bloodletting. After attaching, the tick secretes a protein-rich cementing substance that helps keep itself in place. This patch of cement, which resembles a small chunk of your skin, can often be seen when a tick is removed. As the tick feeds, it releases saliva that contains special compounds that thin the blood and suppress pain.

electron microscope image of black-legged or deer tick mouthparts

How Afraid Should I Be?

Tick bites can cause some discomfort, such as itching or a rash, but they are not a major threat alone. However, in the past 25 years, ticks have become more of a concern as they have been found to carry serious diseases.

So let's look at a few of the tick-borne diseases and where they are usually found. In the Southwest, 5 tick-borne illnesses have been reported: Rocky Mountain spotted fever, tick-borne relapsing fever, Lyme disease, tick paralysis and tularemia.

ROCKY MOUNTAIN SPOTTED FEVER

Rocky Mountain spotted fever (RMSF) is a tick-borne disease found in the Southwest; however, it is very rare. Transmitted primarily by the American dog tick, and sometimes by the Rocky Mountain wood tick, the most common symptom for this disease is a small spotted rash that occurs first on the palms of the hands or the soles of the feet; the rash then spreads to other parts of the body. Muscle pain and fever are additional common symptoms. Even though it is easily treatable, RMSF is often misdiagnosed because people don't realize the disease is present in that area.

TICK-BORNE RELAPSING FEVER

Tick-borne relapsing fever (TBRF) is an infection caused by a bacterium which is found in ticks that feed on rodents. TBRF can only be spread if an infected tick bites you. Like Rocky Mountain spotted fever, the disease is very rare in the Southwest, but cases have been reported in every state in the region.

Symptoms may include a sudden fever, chills, headaches, muscle or joint aches, nausea, and a rash may also occur. These symptoms continue for 2–9 days and then disappear. This cycle may continue for several weeks if the person is not treated with the appropriate antibiotics. Untreated, TBRF can cause serious complications, particularly among young children and the elderly.

black-legged or deer tick

LYME DISEASE

Most cases of Lyme disease occur outside the Southwest, and while Lyme disease is extremely uncommon in the area, it's a serious disease that merits attention.

Lyme disease is caused by a bacterium called a spirochete (spy-row-keet). Spirochetes can only be transmitted when a tick bites a host and remains attached for more than 48 hours. Seventy to ninety percent of patients infected with Lyme disease develop a circular, red "bull's-eye" rash at the site of the bite. Left untreated, Lyme disease can be serious, affecting the skin, joints, heart and nervous system. Thankfully, antibiotics are often effective; the earlier antibiotics are administered, the greater the likelihood of successful treatment.

The Centers for Disease Control (CDC) estimates that only 10–20 percent of Lyme disease cases are reported. Even so, over 30,000 new cases were diagnosed nationally last year and the rate of infection is increasing.

TICK PARALYSIS

Tick paralysis is a disease that sometimes occurs when ticks—most commonly the Rocky Mountain wood tick—remain attached to a person for an extended period. Caused by a neurotoxin in the tick's saliva, symptoms include difficulty walking, numbness in the legs and arms and difficulty in breathing. A doctor should always address breathing difficulties. Children are most susceptible to tick paralysis and may also display flu-like symptoms. The paralysis starts lower in the body and moves its way up. Fortunately, once the tick is removed, the condition is reversible and recovery is rapid.

TULAREMIA

Tularemia, also known as rabbit fever, is an infectious disease caused by a bacterium usually associated with rabbits and hares, but it is sometimes present in other small mammals. Humans can acquire the bacterium when bitten by an infected tick (or deer fly; see page 52), after handling infected animal carcasses, or by ingesting the bacterium in contaminated food or water. Most people acquire the illness from a tick, an insect bite or after coming into contact with the blood of infected animals. It is not communicable.

THINK TWICE

Think twice before letting your dog or cat indoors without a good tick check after an outing in the woods or grasslands during tick season. Neglecting your pet might simply allow a host of uninvited ticks into your home.

Tularemia symptoms vary depending on how the bacterium is acquired, and can include fever, chills, headaches, muscle aches, joint pain, dry cough, progressive weakness and pneumonia (if the bacterium is inhaled). If contaminated blood comes into contact with skin, symptoms can include ulcers on the skin. If infected meat is ingested, symptoms could include a sore throat, upset stomach, diarrhea and vomiting.

Preventing Tick Bites

- Prevent ticks from getting to your skin by wearing appropriate clothing, such as long pants with the cuffs tucked into shin-high socks or boots. Light-colored clothing makes it easier to spot a hitchhiking tick.

- Limit your time in tall grass and brushy areas, particularly in the spring and fall.

- Chemical warfare on ticks can help. A 0.5 percent concentration of permethrin sprayed on your pants and shirt can be very effective. Note it is important that you don't spray permethrin on your skin. Some folks claim that spraying a mosquito repellent with a high concentration of DEET (N, N-diethyl-meta-toluamide) on their clothes also repels ticks.

dog or wood tick

- Perform diligent tick checks after outings. If appropriate, ask for help in checking hard-to-see spots, such as your back.

So you find a fastened tick. Now what?

- Simply put, the longer a tick feeds on you, the greater the odds of it transmitting a tick-borne illness such as Lyme disease. Immediate tick removal lessens the risk of infection.

- To properly remove a tick, it is best to grasp it with a fine tweezers, but fingers will do the job. Do not use petroleum jelly, gasoline, nail polish remover or a hot match.

- Grasp the tick as close to the point of attachment as possible and pull straight up, gently but firmly. Do not jerk or twist the tick, and don't squeeze it, since that might push infectious substances into the wound.

- Don't worry if the tick's mouthparts remain in the skin. Your body will reject the foreign material and be rid of it in a few days. The bite might become reddish and even warm to the touch, but that's a normal reaction.

- After the tick is removed, disinfect the skin thoroughly and wash your hands with soap and water.

- While it might be difficult to determine how long the tick has been fastened, it will help if you recall a situation when you might have picked up a tick, such as a hike in the woods, camping or petting a dog that had recently been outdoors. This information will be particularly helpful should you later require medical treatment.

Treatment of Bites

- Watch the bite site for a possible secondary infection or infectious rash for up to 30 days. If you experience persistent headaches or fever within 3–4 days after a tick bite is discovered, it's a good idea to get it checked out.

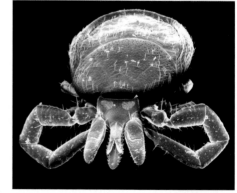

electron microscope image of black-legged or deer tick

- Female fire ant larvae that are fed a high-protein diet become egg-producing queens. Such a diet requires nearly 120,000 visits by food-carrying workers!

Thanks to Fire Ants

- Their tunneling mixes and aerates the soil, in some places replacing the activity of earthworms.

- Fire ants consume large numbers of insects and other arthropods that are harmful to agricultural crops such as cotton, soybeans, peanuts and corn.

Myth Busters

MYTH: Feeding grits or oatmeal to fire ants will cause them to bloat and blow up when they fart.

Ants don't experience flatulence. Even if they did, most ants cannot eat solid foods. Only fire ant larvae can digest solid food; after eating, the larvae immediately regurgitate the nutrients in a liquid, feeding the adult worker ants. These ants, in turn, feed other ants in the colony. On the average, each worker ant will feed 10 other ants. Sharing food through regurgitation is called trophallaxis.

MYTH: Fire ants will kill and devour any living animal in their path.

This kind of statement is born from science fiction movies. Fire ants are primarily omnivores that obtain most of their food by scavenging.

Why They Sting

Fire ants sting only to capture food and defend their colony.

How They Sting

If disturbed, a fire ant colony erupts and hundreds of ants swarm to attack the intruder, no matter the species. Fire ants actually bite prior to stinging; their 2 powerful jaws serve to anchor it on the intruder, allowing the fire ant to drive the tiny barbed stinger found on its abdomen into the intruder's flesh.

The bite is not nearly as painful as the sting, which contains venom that causes the body to release histamine; this causes the pain, swelling and redness one feels after a sting. Oftentimes a small blister will form within 6–24 hours. Unlike honeybees, fire ants can sting repeatedly. If fire ants are not brushed off, they will likely cause up to a dozen or so pus-filled blisters.

The venom is a valuable tool in helping the ant kill prey. The natural chemicals can penetrate an insect's exoskeleton.

How Afraid Should I Be?

A sting causes a very uncomfortable burning sensation, and if you encounter a swarm of fire ants, there's a chance you'll be stung. For most people, fire ant stings are not a serious medical concern; however, very severe cases might require skin grafts.

Some people are allergic to fire ant stings. For those who are, a sting is a medical emergency and can lead to anaphylactic shock and even death. Fire ant stings cause a few deaths each year, but deaths aren't caused by the fire ant's venom. Instead, deaths occur because of anaphylactic shock, an immune system response to the sting. It's ironic that small insects like bees, wasps and ants cause more human deaths each year in the U.S. than venomous snakes and lizards, which are much larger and more feared.

THINK TWICE

Think twice about where you spread out your picnic blanket or set up camp. Be sure to inspect the area for fire ant mounds.

Think twice about scratching any fire ant stings. Rubbing and scratching open blisters often results in a nasty infection.

After any insect sting you should monitor your symptoms, as a sting might require immediate medical attention. The following symptoms are indications of an allergic reaction: headache, dizziness, nausea, sweating, loss of consciousness, coughing, breathing difficulty, hives, reduced heart rate and low blood pressure. If a sting causes these symptoms, seek medical help immediately.

Preventing Fire Ant Stings

- Avoiding encounters is the best prevention. Learn to identify fire ant nests and avoid them. If you locate an ant mound, don't disturb it. If you accidentally step on an ant mound, move away as quickly as possible. Brush off all the ants on your clothing and shoes. Most importantly, teach children these same practices.

- Applying talcum powder around your ankles makes it very difficult for ants to reach your legs.

- If fire ants show up in your yard, consider using a granulated ant killer containing fipronil around the nest. Worker ants carry the pesticide to the colony, thereby destroying the entire colony. If at all possible, *avoid* treating areas where other ant species live. By removing nontarget ant species, you actually make it more difficult to remove fire ants, as these other ants compete with fire ants for food and territory, curbing the growth of fire ant populations.

- On a smaller scale, some people have luck controlling fire ants by pouring boiling water over a mound right after a rain, as fire ant colonies are concentrated during a rain.

Treatment of Stings

- If you are stung in an arm or a leg, elevate the area and apply ice. If blisters appear, carefully clean the sting site with cool water and soap without breaking the blisters.

- An immediate treatment is to apply a solution of 50 percent bleach and 50 percent water to the wound. If applied soon after a bite, this can reduce pain and itching. Stings can also be treated with a paste of meat tenderizer and water; enzymes in the mix can break down some of the venom.

- Minimizing itching reduces the likelihood of secondary infection. If itching is really bothering you, nonprescription cortisone creams can help.

- Most importantly, if any symptoms of anaphylactic shock occur, seek medical attention immediately.

BOTTOM LINE

Red imported fire ants are very aggressive ants capable of inflicting great pain. Learn to recognize their mounds and steer clear of them.

Mosquitoes

According to the Thompson River Indians of British Columbia, Thunder asked Mosquito why he was so fat, and Mosquito replied that he sucked on trees. He didn't want to admit that he really fed on people, because he didn't want Thunder to eat up all the people and deny him of his prey. Mosquito's plan worked very well, and his story explains why Thunder now shoots trees instead of people.

—*Legends of the Earth, Sea, and Sky: An Encyclopedia of Nature Myths* by Tamra Andrews

About Mosquitoes

It is estimated that there are over 2,500 mosquito species in the world. In the Southwest, it is estimated that there are approximately 50 species of mosquitoes. In certain parts of this region, they are easily one of the most abundant biters you'll encounter outdoors. Taken alone, a single mosquito doesn't seem all that intimidating. But what the mosquito lacks in stature, it makes up in numbers and fearless tenacity. Swarms of droning mosquitoes have chased countless picnickers and campers indoors, and they've even driven wanted criminals out of hiding. Fortunately, there's no need to let them ruin your outdoor adventures.

Life and Times . . .

Mosquitoes (genus *Culex*) are members of the order Diptera. Considered "true flies," they are related to houseflies and midges. Mosquitoes have 2 scaled wings, 6 long legs and, of course, a long, piercing proboscis (or beak).

Female mosquitoes lay 200–400 eggs in quiet marshes, swamps, or ponds and in other places that hold stagnant water, such as ditches, old tires and hoof prints. The eggs hatch within days. The tiny larva hangs upside down (like the letter "J") at the surface of the water. It feeds almost continuously on microscopic plant fragments.

About a dozen days later the larva changes (pupates) into the adult mosquito. The pupal covering begins to fill with air until the skin splits open and out emerges the wobbly adult mosquito. It stands and rests on the surface of its watery home for about a half an hour before it flies to nearby grass or brush.

Fascinating Facts

- Only female mosquitoes bite.

- Male mosquitoes feed on rotting fruit or nectar from flowers.

- The female's wings beat 250–500 times per second; the male's feathery antennae help him pick up their species-specific frequency and pitch.

- Mosquitoes are capable of mating within 2 days of hatching. A female mosquito mates only once in her life. She will receive all the sperm needed to produce up to 400 eggs.

Thanks to Mosquitoes

- Mosquitoes are a main food source for other insects and wildlife such as ducklings and young fish. A single little brown bat may eat 5,000 mosquitoes in 1 night!

- Their larvae voraciously process tons of rotting plants (detritus) in wetlands.

- Mosquitoes are important plant pollinators in the Southwest.

Myth Busters

MYTH: All mosquitoes are alike and can be controlled the same way.

There are more than 170 mosquito species in North America alone, and different species exhibit different behaviors. Some feed just before nightfall, while others feed around the clock or whenever a host is near. Timing is essential when targeting the winged adults, as chemical spraying is most effective when meteorological conditions such as wind and humidity are favorable.

MYTH: Bug zappers are effective against mosquitoes.

Researchers found that while ultraviolet or black light bug zappers do attract and kill thousands of insects within a 24-hour period, only 6.4 percent of a 5-day catch consists of mosquitoes. Of that, only half of the mosquitoes killed were the blood-feeding females. This is clearly not a good choice for controlling mosquitoes.

MYTH: The mosquito dies after she takes a blood meal.

Mosquitoes are capable of biting more than once. After the female mosquito takes a blood meal she completes the development of her eggs and may deposit up to 200 of them at a time. She may seek another blood meal and lay again.

Why They Bite

Mosquitoes require the proteins found in the blood of warm-blooded animals to produce eggs, which assure there will be future generations of mosquitoes. As the most numerous mammals on the planet, humans are a big part of the mosquito's dinner buffet.

How They Bite

The female mosquito uses sight to locate a warm-blooded host; females also can detect the host's body heat, as well as the carbon dioxide released during respiration. Once she finds a host, she pierces its skin and releases an anticoagulant (a blood thinner) into the host. Proteins found in the insect's saliva create the itch and welt after the mosquito bites.

How Afraid Should I Be?

Mosquito-borne diseases, such as malaria, are a serious threat in much of the world. Thankfully, in the Southwest, mosquito bites are mostly just a painful irritation. With that said, residents living here should be aware of the recent arrival of West Nile Virus (WNV) in the region. Human cases of the virus have been reported in every state in the region. It has also reportedly been found in a few dead birds and mosquito samples in southern California.

WEST NILE VIRUS

- Mosquitoes are the main vectors of WNV, which interferes with the central nervous system and causes inflammation of brain tissue. A mosquito may become infected with the virus by feeding on infected birds; if an infected mosquito bites a human or animal, the virus may be injected into the new host.

- Your risk of becoming seriously ill from WNV is very low. Even in areas where the virus is circulating, very few mosquitoes are infected. And fewer than 1 in 150 people who are bitten and become infected get severely ill. People over 50 years old and the chronically ill are at the highest risk of developing severe symptoms.

- Most people infected with WNV will not show symptoms. Others might experience mild symptoms such as fever, headache, nausea or vomiting and sometimes swollen lymph glands or a skin rash on the torso. Mild symptoms can last from a few days to several weeks. Severe symptoms include high fever, headache, stupor, coma, vision loss, numbness and paralysis. These symptoms might last for several weeks, and the effects could be permanent.

At the time of this writing, there have been no cases of eastern equine encephalitis or western equine encephalitis among humans in the Southwest.

Preventing Mosquito Bites

PHYSICAL BARRIERS

The most effective means of dealing with mosquitoes is to put a barrier between yourself and the insect.

- Limit your time outdoors at dusk and dawn, when mosquitoes are most active.

- Wear loose-fitting, light-colored clothes that allow air movement but prevent the probing of mosquitoes. Dark clothing attracts mosquitoes.

- Head nets and bug jackets made of fine mesh keep insects from reaching your skin, yet allow air movement. Some are made to absorb repellents.

- Use screen tents to enclose picnic tables and lawn chairs.

NATURAL MOSQUITO REPELLENTS

- Oil of lemon eucalyptus repels mosquitoes. Citronella can work too, but must be applied more often than synthetic chemicals. Some people claim success using Avon Skin-So-Soft, while others believe eating a clove of raw garlic each day will give their skin an odor that keeps mosquitoes away. (Their friends probably stay away too!)

- Outdoor products, such as mosquito coils or citronella candles or torches, can create uncomfortable air space for mosquitoes.

CHEMICAL REPELLENTS

- The most common and effective repellent ingredient is DEET (N, N-diethyl-meta-toluamide). However, it can cause eye and sinus irritation, headaches, insomnia and confusion. Repellents with high DEET concentrations can melt some synthetic materials, dissolve paint and leave bad odors.

- Permethrin is a synthetic broad-spectrum insecticide. Your skin metabolizes, or breaks down, permethrin in less than 20 minutes after contact. When applied to clothing, it can last for hours.

event that a spider gets into your bed, it will not seek to bite you. If you happen to roll onto one, it might bite, but it's not likely.

According to some emergency room personnel, unexplained swelling or skin irritation is often blamed on a "spider bite." Nevertheless, when patients are asked if they actually saw a spider, they almost always say no. Research has shown that over 80 percent of suspected spider bites are caused by other insects, ticks or medical conditions.

Why They Bite

The primary reason a spider bites is to kill its prey, and almost all species of spiders are venomous. The venom helps them quickly kill or paralyze their prey. When a spider bites a human, it is not interested in wrapping you in silk; it is strictly a defensive act. Spiders are generally very timid around humans and will skitter away quickly if disturbed.

THINK TWICE

Think twice before calling a daddy longlegs a spider. They are nonvenomous arachnids that belong to a group called harvestmen.

Think twice about stepping on a spider caught indoors. By carefully catching and releasing the spider outside, you will model caring behavior to your children and others.

Around the world there is a universal belief that it is unlucky to kill a spider. In fact, there is an old English rhyme that speaks to such compassion toward spiders: "If you wish to live and thrive, let a spider run alive."

How They Bite

Actually, spiders don't bite, they inject. The spider's mouth is located directly below its eyes. Their large jaws are called chelicerae, and these vertical structures are often lined with small teeth and tipped with 2 fangs. In most spiders, these jaws swing inward from the sides to grasp prey. In some larger spider species, the jaws swing downward to pin down prey.

A spider's venom is secreted through the fangs in the prey, but spiders less than $5/16$ of an inch can't bite you, as they are too small. Pretty much all spiders larger than $5/16$ of an inch can bite humans, but most usually *won't*. Those that can break your skin will sometimes inject harmless venom, and some will not inject venom at all. Most spider bites are less painful than a bee sting, but some people are more sensitive to bites than others.

How Afraid Should I Be?

In the Southwest it is primarily the widow and brown recluse spiders that are capable of delivering nasty bites. A very shy group of species, the widow spiders are typically not aggressive but they will both bite when accidentally trapped, disturbed or threatened. Usually they prefer to retreat. The most common of the widow spiders in this region is the western black widow spider.

black widow

Widow spiders are often found hanging upside down in their tangled webs. The female delivers the more serious, but rarely lethal, bite. She has a round, shiny black abdomen with a red hourglass-shaped marking on the underside of her belly. Her bite might feel like a pinprick. The bite site might swell slightly and bear faint red marks. Within a few hours the pain intensifies and stiffness begins. Other symptoms of the neurotoxic venom include chills, fever, nausea and severe abdominal pain.

The hobo spider is another species to be aware of in the Southwest region. This widespread spider has its origins in Europe and gets its name from its habit of hitching rides from place to place. It has a larger body than the black widow, long legs and 2 appendages that resemble boxing gloves (these are actually sex organs).

hobo

The hobo spider constructs a web that looks like a funnel. Like widow spiders, the hobo prefers to flee when disturbed. The hobo spider is slightly venomous, but it is not a spider to be feared. When biting, it often injects no venom; this is called a dry bite. If venom is injected, the bite will turn red and swell.

brown recluse

The brown recluse spider delivers the most dangerous bite in the United States. It is *not* native to the Southwest. However, there have been rare incidents where brown recluse spiders have accidentally been transported miles from their normal range in cargo. Colored tan to dark brown, it is approximately 1/2 inch long. It bears a distinctive, dark violin-shaped marking on top of the front body section (cephalothorax) and has 3 pairs of eyes. Almost all other species of spiders in this region have 4 pairs of eyes.

Several hours after a somewhat painless bite, a blister forms and the surrounding skin begins to darken and swell. The venom of the brown recluse can cause extensive tissue damage. It normally takes up to 2 months for such a bite to heal.

Preventing Spider Bites

- Avoid handling spiders with your bare hands. When removing spiders from your home, gently cover them with a glass or jar, slide a piece of paper underneath and release them outdoors.

- Don't reach into dusty, dark recesses with your bare hands.

Treatment of Bites

- If possible, capture the biting spider so it can be properly identified. In the highly unlikely event that a widow spider bites you, capture it for positive identification and seek immediate medical attention.

- Clean and wash the bite site with soap and hot water. Apply ice and elevate the affected area.

- To guard against infection, apply an antiseptic lotion or cream.

- Most bites improve within a few hours to 3 days.

- Seek medical attention if symptoms persist or worsen. This is especially important with children.

BOTTOM LINE

Spiders are timid around people and skitter away if disturbed. If one does bite you, it is strictly in self-defense. In the Southwest, most spider bites are harmless, but if a widow spider or a brown recluse spider bites you, seek medical attention immediately.

Deer and Horse Flies

Every summer, I shudder when I hear the simple declaration, "The deer flies are out." Along with horse flies, these persistent biters can turn an otherwise perfect day at the beach, in the garden, or in the boat into a sore test of endurance.

Sometimes, though, they help us see the larger drama of life. I recall one day in my garden as I crawled down a row of peas, deer flies flew laps around my head and occasionally stole in for a quick bite. Suddenly I heard a clattering of wings just above my head. I tipped my head to sneak a peek. A dragonfly! Soon a second joined it. I heard more clattering and even felt slight taps on my hat. They were picking off deer flies that were alighting on my head! In a sense, I had become a dragonfly feeder. By attracting the deer flies, I provided easy pickings for the predators. What had been a pest to me was sustenance for the dragonflies.

About Deer and Horse Flies

This is a well-represented group of flies. There are approximately 4,300 species in the world, with more than 160 species of horse flies and over 110 types of deer flies occurring in the continental United States. Both deer and horse flies have similar life cycles.

deer fly

horse fly

Deer flies, sometimes called yellow flies, are smaller than horse flies. They measure about $^1/_4$ to $^3/_8$ inch long. They are commonly tan colored with distinct dark patches on their wings. Their antennae are slightly longer than the heads. They are strong fliers and are usually not solitary.

The larger horse fly averages $^1/_2$ to $1^1/_4$ inches long and is more robust. Its wings have no patches and are uniformly cloudy. The antennae are shorter than the head and thick at the base. Horse fly eyes are large and appear colorful.

Both flies are dependent on wetlands, such as marshes, ponds, watering holes or slow-moving streams, for their life cycles. As adults, they can cover wide areas. Both types of flies are particularly fond of the combination of wetlands and swales and brush. In the Southwest, they are most common at higher elevations and less a problem in the hot and arid habitats of the region.

Life and Times . . .

In the Southwest, deer flies typically make their appearance in late spring to early summer. Prior to mating, males and females feed on plant nectars and

juices. After mating, the female seeks a meal of blood.

Males are rarely seen but can be distinguished from females by their large compound eyes, which touch each other; the female's eyes are distinctly separate.

The female lays a single mass of 100–800 eggs on the underside of a leaf or

deer fly laying eggs

on the stem of a plant growing out of a wetland. Freshly laid egg masses are whitish and soon darken upon exposure to air.

In 2–3 days, the eggs hatch and the larvae drop down into the water or mud to complete their development. The last larval stage spends the winter dormant in the wetland. The following spring, the larvae shed their skin and proceed to the pupal stage. It takes 1–3 weeks for the adult fly to pupate. Most deer and horse flies pupate on the edge of marshes, swamps and ponds.

The larvae of deer flies feed on insects and plant material. On the other hand, all studied species of horse fly larvae eat other insects.

Fascinating Facts

- Only female deer and horse flies bite.

- The mating flight for these flies is generally in the early morning. The female requires a blood meal only after mating.

- Some of the larger species of horse flies require 2–3 years to develop in an aquatic environment before emerging as adults.

Thanks to Deer and Horse Flies

- Both of these flies are important prey species for many birds and other insects.

- The aquatic larvae of deer and horse flies provide a food source for many species of fish.

- The males of each species are important plant pollinators.

Myth Busters

MYTH: Swatting at deer flies will chase them away.

It won't. In fact, the motion will agitate them and probably attract more.

Why They Bite

With some exceptions, the female deer or horse fly needs to feed on blood in order to produce viable eggs. Like all other biting flies, they only bite during daylight hours—lying in ambush in the shade of brush or trees and swarming around any passing potential host. They zero in on a target by noting movement, the release of carbon dioxide (emitted when you exhale) and odors such as fragrant perfumes or shampoos.

How They Bite

Deer and horse fly bites are painfully similar. A tiny pair of blade-like mandibles lacerate the skin, causing blood to flow—which is lapped up with a spongelike mouthpart. Like mosquitoes, these flies incorporate an anticoagulant into the bite to make the wound bleed more freely. A bite often results in a small red welt that might persist for several days. Slight swelling and itchiness may occur at the site of the bite.

If deer or horse flies are numerous enough, they will change your outdoor

horse fly

plans. Of the 2 species of flies, I consider the deer fly a greater pest because they are rarely alone in their attack, whereas horse flies tend to be more solitary.

How Afraid Should I Be?

Deer and horse fly bites are generally not serious injuries. But they can result in open wounds and a possible secondary infection. Aggressively scratching the affected area can make matters worse.

Even if deer flies only occasionally bite you, they are extremely annoying as they swirl in a horde around your head. Ironically, they seem to flock to moving targets. In other words, if you restrict your movements, you will be less of a target. Luckily, neither species will enter your tent or home to seek you out. If you have ever noticed a wayward deer or horse fly in a house or vehicle, they are usually bouncing off a window trying to get out.

THINK TWICE

Think twice about strolling into the brush or hiking near a wetland during fly season. Whatever you do, don't forget your hat!

And think twice about being the first person in line when on a hike . . . you will receive more of the flies' wrath than those following.

At elevations higher than 3,000 feet in the Southwest, it is possible to encounter deer flies infected with the bacteria that causes the disease tularemia. Known sometimes as rabbit or deer fly fever, tularemia is an infectious disease that is often associated with rabbits and hares. Other small mammals can carry the bacterium, which lives in their system. Tularemia can be passed to humans through an infected deer fly or tick bite or through handling an infected rabbit carcass.

Rabbit hunters should wear impervious gloves when they skin and gut their game. The meat should also be thoroughly cooked. Tularemia cannot be spread from person to person. Tularemia symptoms can include chills, fever, headaches, muscle aches, joint pain and a dry cough. If you suspect you were exposed to tularemia bacteria, promptly see a doctor. Tularemia is effectively treated with antibiotics for a period of 10–14 days.

Preventing Deer and Horse Fly Bites

- The best prevention for keeping both of these biting flies at bay is to cover up. When deer fly season is underway, I don't leave home without a hat.

- Repellents do not work.

- Avoid deer and horse fly habitat during midsummer.

- Some outdoor workers and enthusiasts have good success with deer fly adhesive patches. Nontoxic and odorless, the double-sided patches work like portable fly strips. Press one to the back of your hat or cap and it will attract circling deer flies—which find themselves stuck upon landing.

- Deer flies typically go after the tallest person in a group, as well as the one walking in front. Use this tip wisely. If the hike leader turns to you complaining about the deer flies, swing your hands wildly at imaginary antagonists and grumble loudly!

- I have had some success sticking the stems of foliage down the back of my shirt, so the front projects like an umbrella above my head. This creates a canopy of ferns over my head that does a decent job of distracting the deer flies. I think it looks cool, too.

- I have a neighbor who swears that affixing a blue—yes, blue—Dixie cup to the top of her head attracts deer flies to the cup instead of her head. (I'll stick to ferns, myself.)

Treatment of Bites

Wash bites with warm water and soap. Benadryl and other anti-itch or anti-inflammatory compounds, lotions and creams can provide itching relief.

BOTTOM LINE

Deer and horse fly bites are slightly painful but generally not dangerous. The bite may produce a small red welt accompanied by minor swelling and itching that lasts several days, but these harassing flies cannot bite you if they can't get to your skin. Wearing a hat, a long-sleeved shirt and long pants can help prevent most bites.

Hornets, Wasps and Yellow Jackets

No group of insects urges humans to retreat faster than wasps, hornets and yellow jackets. They wear their stripes well. We have come to learn that the distinct pattern of belted stripes encircling the bodies of this fierce crew is a clear visual warning to "Watch Out!" While most encounters are benign, their stings are painful and, for some people, allergic reactions to the venom can be life-threatening.

About Hornets, Wasps and Yellow Jackets

Like honeybees and bumblebees, these groups of thin-waisted and mostly hairless insects live in social colonies made up of workers (infertile females), queens and males.

Of the approximately 15,000 species of stinging wasps in the world, 95 percent do not sting humans. Wasps, particularly yellow jackets, are more aggressive than honeybees. In the Southwest, yellow jackets are not common in dry and hot areas. Hornets and yellow jackets tend to live at higher elevations.

Tarantula wasps, also known as tarantula hawks, are a nonsocial group of wasps that target tarantulas to complete their unique life cycle. Striking in appearance, the tarantula wasp is robust (up to 2 inches long) and has a metallic blue body and orange wings; it was deemed the official state insect of New Mexico in 1998.

The female tarantula wasp stings a spider and injects it with a paralyzing venom. She then utilizes an existing burrow or digs a new one to bury the paralyzed spider. Before she entombs the spider, she lays a single egg on the spider's abdomen. Later, when the egg hatches, the tiny wasp larvae will ingest the spider's innards. Of course, the spider dies as the wasp grows and continues to feed.

bald-faced hornet

paper wasp

yellow jacket

tarantula wasp

Life and Times . . .

Colonies of hornets, wasps and yellow jackets remain active for only 1 summer, after which the fertilized queens fly away to start more colonies. Other colony members die at the end of the summer, and the nest is not reused.

Fertilized queens winter in protected places such as hollow logs, stumps, under bark, in leaf litter, in abandoned animal dens and in man-made structures. They emerge in the warm days of late April and early May to select a nest site and build a small paper nest in which to lay their eggs.

After her first brood hatches, a queen feeds the young larvae for about 18–20 days. These young will eventually pupate and emerge around mid-June as the colony's first group of workers. Infertile females, their jobs will include foraging for food, defending the nest, and caring for the queen's subsequent hatches of larvae. Each cell in the nest may be used for 2 or 3 batches of broods.

The larvae's primary diet consists of protein-rich foods such as insects, meats and fish. Adults are particularly fond of fruit, flower nectar and tree sap, which provide ample doses of sugars and carbohydrates.

The queen stays with her nest throughout the summer, laying eggs. Eventually she might build an empire of several thousand workers. In late August and early September, she creates cells where future queens and males are produced. They are cared for and fed by the sterile workers before leaving the colony in the fall for a mating flight. After mating, the males die and fertilized queens look for protected sites to spend the winter. The old queen from the summer nest dies, and the workers begin to behave erratically until social order breaks down. With the onset of winter, the remaining colony dies.

BALD-FACED HORNET IDENTIFICATION

The bald-faced hornet is similar to a paper wasp and the yellow jacket. Two primary differences involve the hornet's nest and physical appearance.

- The bald-faced hornet's nest is ball- or oval-shaped and can be larger than a basketball. Nests are most often constructed on a tree limb or shrub branch. Hidden by summer foliage, they are most easily viewed after the leaves fall in autumn.

bald-faced hornet nest

- The hornet itself is large, black and thin waisted. It is named for its distinctive white or "bald" face.

paper wasp nest

PAPER WASP IDENTIFICATION

The queen paper wasp creates a single layer of cells that is attached by a stem to the underside of eaves, benches and other protected overhangs.

Paper wasps, like yellow jackets, are striped in yellow and black. However, they are slightly larger (particularly in the abdomen) than yellow jackets.

YELLOW JACKET IDENTIFICATION

Of the 3 groups mentioned here, yellow jackets are the only ones that often nest underground. Sometimes they nest behind the siding of a building or in a building crevice.

yellow jacket underground nest

Fascinating Facts

- Wasps and hornets make their papery nests by chewing on tiny pieces of wood, bark or even cardboard. They add their saliva to the chewed wood and "paint" it into a smooth, thin material used for making the nest. The various colors of the rather artful nest are determined by the source of the wood.

- After the nests freeze in the fall, any remaining larvae are dead. These frozen treats are high in fat and are desirable food items for squirrels, skunks and even birds such as woodpeckers and blue jays.

- The stinger on this group of insects has evolved from the long, sharp portion of the insect called the ovipositor. It is also the mechanism from which eggs are deposited.

Thanks to Hornets, Wasps and Yellow Jackets

- Worker wasps and hornets feed on caterpillars and other insects that are often harmful to human food crops. These include corn earworms, army worms, tobacco hornworms, house flies, blowflies and harmful caterpillars.

- Although they lack the pollen-carrying structures of bees, yellow jackets can be minor pollinators when visiting flowers.

- They often eat the flesh of dead animals, making them important members of the cleanup crew.

Myth Busters

MYTH: All bees and wasps sting.

Many wasps are non-stinging and most do not sting humans. Only female wasps are capable of inflicting a sting. Males are rarely seen since their function is to mate during the fall mating flight. And just because a wasp or a hornet looks scary doesn't mean it will sting you. The ichneumon wasp has a long ovipositor (a tube for depositing eggs) at the end of its body, which looks a lot like a stinger, but it's not. The wasp drills the ovipositor into soft or rotting wood and lays its eggs.

Myth: Just because an insect looks like a wasp or hornet, it is one.

Actually, many harmless insects look a lot like wasps or hornets. Many insect species mimic the colors of their feistier neighbors in order to protect themselves. If an insect looks like a yellow jacket, wasp or hornet, birds and other predators think twice before attacking, as the predators see the bright

bald-faced hornet

colors and sometimes shy away. But many innocent insects are often confused for wasps or hornets and unfairly swatted. Just because an insect looks like a wasp or a hornet, it doesn't mean it is one.

Why They Sting

These groups of insects sting primarily to kill prey. They are predators. Secondly, they use the sting to defend themselves or the colony. They simply do not seek out humans to randomly sting. With that said, while your intentions might be totally innocent, if a hornet, wasp or yellow jacket perceives you as a threat, it will sting you.

How They Sting

The stinger is located in the tip of the abdomen. Unlike honeybees—which can only sting once—hornets, wasps and yellow jackets do not lose their stinger and can sting repeatedly. The dose of toxin delivered is less than that of a honeybee and is reduced with each sting. When a hornet, a wasp or a yellow jacket stings, the 2 halves of the abdomen casing open up to allow the stinger to emerge. The stinger is made up of a piercing stylet and 2 tiny flanking lancets.

The sting is delivered when the stinger is thrust into the victim and the micro-lancets move back and forth like a saw. These lancets are slightly barbed at the edges. Anchored in the flesh, the moving lancets trigger a pumping action at the end of the abdomen, causing the venom sac to pump venom into the wound. Since hornets, wasps and yellow jackets have smaller barbs on their lancets than honeybees, they can pull the shaft out and fly happily away. On the other hand, the honeybee's stinger stays fixed in the flesh. When it pulls away, it literally pulls out the stinger and venom sac. The injury results in the bee's death.

The sting of hornets contains acetylcholine, which stimulates pain nerves more than the stings of other wasps, so hornet stings can be a bit more painful.

How Afraid Should I Be?

There is no need to fear these insects. Respect, yes, but not fear. Most of their lives are spent trying to survive, searching for food for themselves and the brood. Any attack on you is time spent away from foraging.

Minimize attacks through avoidance, staying calm and being alert. For example, in late summer, foraging yellow jackets become a nuisance when they

THINK TWICE

Think twice about aggressively shooing away hornets, wasps or yellow jackets from your picnic. Flailing your arms and swinging at the insect might provoke defensive behavior and that could result in a sting.

Think twice about trying to kill a hornet, wasp or yellow jacket that you discover while driving your car. Slowly pull over to the side of the road and open the windows and doors so it can fly out. You are in far more danger of initiating a car accident if you try to get the insect out while you're behind the wheel.

change from eating meat to a diet of ripe, rotting fruit, human garbage, sweet drinks and picnic foods.

The sting of the tarantula wasp can be very painful, though it is usually short-lived. Unlike most other social wasps, which often sting when defending their colony, the solitary tarantula wasp stings when it feels threatened and you almost have to try to be stung to get nailed by one of these oversized wasps.

By understanding their behavior and responding accordingly, we can prevent most attacks.

paper wasp

Preventing Stings

- Hornets, wasps and particularly yellow jackets are very defensive around their nests. If you locate nests, simply note them and avoid them, telling other people who frequent the area. I would not recommend nest eradication unless the nest poses a threat to humans. I have had very good success in preventing wasp nest construction by applying a thin film of petroleum jelly underneath picnic tabletops and seats, deck benches, etc. If you must get rid of a nest, plan to remove it early in the morning or later in the evening, when cooler temperatures have ushered the inhabitants into the nest. If you are using a chemical, read and carefully follow the label directions.

- Avoid fragrant soaps, shampoos, perfumes, aftershaves and colognes. Hornets, wasps and yellow jackets are sometimes attracted to them.

- Keep children from throwing rocks at nests or spraying them with water. Avoid making loud noises or disturbing the nests.

- Some folks have luck with yellow jacket/hornet traps that are placed outside a home or near a picnic site. The sweet bait lures them into the trap, from which there is no exit.

Thanks to Honeybees

- Some plants need honeybee pollination as much as they need water and sunlight. The United States Department of Agriculture estimates that one-third of our daily diet relies on insect pollination, and honeybees perform 80 percent of that pollination.

- Bee venom contains a very potent anti-inflammatory agent and is used by many people to manage joint pain, arthritis and even multiple sclerosis.

- Bees pollinate many types of plants that cause allergy problems for some folks. Some people claim that honey produced from the nectar of these plants' flowers helps minimize the misery.

- Beekeeping is a vital occupation for thousands of people. Bees help produce a variety of products, including honey, pollen and beeswax.

Myth Busters

MYTH: A honeybee can sting you over and over.

When a bee pulls away after stinging you, she pulls away a portion of her abdomen, resulting in her death. She is willing to give up her life to defend herself or the hive.

Why They Sting

Bees sting for 2 primary reasons: to defend themselves and to defend their colony. Like wasps, hornets and yellow jackets, bees do not go out looking for victims to sting.

How They Sting

A bee's stinger is a formidable weapon. It consists of 2 sharp, curved blades with 8–10 barbs near the tip. A narrow duct is formed when the blades are positioned next to each other. This duct serves as the channel from which the venom is delivered from the venom sac. Muscles near the stinger force the barb into the flesh and then muscles pump venom into the wound.

When you are stung, the stinger emits a pheromonal alarm (a mixture of chemical compounds designed to provoke a certain behavior) that is detected by other bees; this quickly warns other bees to maintain alertness and prepare to attack.

How Afraid Should I Be?

Given that honeybees and bumblebees are not normally aggressive and are far more interested in working for the welfare of their hive, they are not usually a problem. However, if you know or suspect you are allergic to bee venom, be proactive and seek a doctor who will prescribe the proper medication. Then it is up to you to have it accessible when outdoors. Most human deaths occur in the first hour after the sting occurs.

honeybee covered with pollen

Preventing Bee Stings

- If a bee is flying around you, simply ignore it or gently urge it away.

- Flailing your arms and swinging at the bee might provoke a defensive behavior, and that could result in a sting.

- Avoid strongly scented skin products, soaps and shampoos.

- If you are working in a flower garden or find yourself anywhere that bees gather, perhaps the best preparation is to simply wear proper clothing that minimizes skin exposure. Mosquito repellents are ineffective against bees.

- Bees sometimes swarm in the most unusual places. Officials at a major league baseball game once had to call a timeout while a beekeeper removed a swarm that had clustered in one of the dugouts!

- Swarms of bees are rarely aggressive, and you should be patient and let them move on their way. Sometimes the swarm can linger for a couple of days. Please *do not* kill them with a pesticide. At the very least, contact a local beekeeper; they will be happy to remove the bees to create a new hive for their beekeeping yard.

Treatment of Stings

- Immediately remove the stinger and venom sac by carefully scraping the stinger with a fingernail or knife blade. *Do not* grasp the stinger with your fingers or a tweezers or you will only force venom into the wound.

- You can also purchase an extractor to remove the venom from the site of the sting. However, most stings do not happen with a first aid kit nearby, and this is the likely place to find a venom extractor.

- Wash the site of the sting with soap and water and apply ice to minimize swelling and pain. Mixing a solution of $1/2$ teaspoon meat tenderizer and 1 teaspoon water and placing it on the wound can minimize discomfort.

- Pay close attention to how you feel after a sting. Allergic reactions to the bee's venom occur in approximately 1 percent of the human population. If someone else is stung, watch them closely and seek immediate medical attention if you notice any change in breathing, if they complain of scratchiness in the throat or exhibit symptoms of hives. In the meantime, keep the victim quiet, calm and as still as possible.

- If you or one of your family members is allergic to bee stings, ask your doctor for a prescription for either an Anaphylaxis Emergency Treatment Kit or an EpiPen. Both contain injectable adrenaline (epinephrine) for allergic reactions. Carry your kit or EpiPen with you at all times during the peak bee season. Carefully follow instructions to administer the epinephrine.

BOTTOM LINE

There is no reason to fear honeybees and bumblebees. They only sting to defend themselves or their colony. When a bee buzzes around you, enjoy the unique "music" of this beneficial little insect, or gently urge it away. Flailing your arms might provoke defensive behavior—and a sting.

Giant Desert Centipedes

If you wanted an excellent monster for a horror movie, you would do well to use the giant desert centipede as a model. It is so alien and ominous looking that it is hard to tell which is the front end and what is the back end. But this agile predator, with its many legs, can deliver a painful bite if you are careless in trying to handle one.

About Giant Desert Centipedes

Of the approximately 2,000 species of centipedes in the world, the giant desert centipede is one of the largest, at 8 inches. At home in the arid areas of the Southwest, this oversized, venomous centipede has an orange body with a black head and tail. For this reason, it is also known as the red-headed centipede. Its pattern of contrasting and highly visible colors serves as a warning that this centipede is not to be messed with.

Life and Times . . .

After a winter of staying inactive underground or beneath rocks, the female giant desert centipede lays her eggs during the warmer months of late spring and summer. She coils around the eggs and tends them by keeping them clean. It is believed that this egg grooming helps ward off mold and bacteria. After hatching, the young do not go through the typical larval and nymph stages that most insects experience; instead they go through a simple metamorphosis. The tiny young resemble adults but have fewer legs. As they grow, they molt their skin and some species of centipedes add another pair of legs with each molting sequence. Within a few days of hatching, the young disperse to fend for themselves.

Giant desert centipedes easily become dehydrated, so during the day they usually seek damp, cool haunts to avoid the scorching desert sun. At night, these surprisingly fast arthropods turn into hunters, seeking prey such as insects, spiders and even small rodents. They kill by grasping the prey, almost coiling around it, and injecting their venom into the victim.

When winter returns, this hardy multi-legged beast seeks shelter and overwinters. They are capable of living for several years.

Fascinating Facts

- Centipedes have only 1 pair of legs on each segment, while millipedes have 2 legs on most body segments. Millipedes are slow-moving scavengers whereas centipedes are fast predators.

- At the tail end of the giant desert centipede there is a "pseudohead," or false head, to confuse potential predators. The pseudohead even has elongated structures that resemble antennae. If the predator mistakenly grabs the pseudohead, the real head is free to bite in defense.

Thanks to Giant Desert Centipedes

- Giant desert centipedes are an important part of the desert food chain and they add to the biological complexity of the desert ecosystem.

- Centipedes should be encouraged to live around a garden because of their role in feeding on other insects, including insects that can be garden pests. Some gardeners provide stones or edges of mulch to encourage the centipedes to live nearby.

Myth Busters

MYTH: Centipedes are bugs (insects).

It's true that insects and centipedes are both arthropods—the biological category (phylum) typified by organisms with articulated, jointed limbs. Even so, there are many types of arthropods, and insects are merely one subcategory of the bigger arthropod family.

Unlike insects, centipedes are equipped with dozens of legs; insects have 6 legs. And while an insect has 3 main body parts, a head, thorax and abdomen, centipedes have many body segments with a pair of legs attached to each segment.

MYTH: All centipedes have 100 legs.

While the centipede's name might imply it has 100 legs, most centipedes have fewer than 50. A pair of legs originates with each centipede body segment.

Why They Bite

They are carnivores and their venom helps them subdue prey such as insects, lizards, frogs and rodents. The venom can also help them defend themselves.

How They Bite

Giant desert centipedes do not bite with their mouth. Instead they use mouthparts for chewing and inject venom with modified claws positioned underneath their head. These claws resemble pincers and evolved from the first pair of legs. The venom dissolves cells and can result in pain and inflammation. Children or elderly people often react more negatively to a bite.

THINK TWICE

Think twice about reaching under rocks or debris out in the desert, centipedes or a venomous snake could be avoiding the hot sun by resting there.

How Afraid Should I Be?

While painful, a bite is not life-threatening and is only as serious as a bee sting. But because the centipede is an opportunistic feeder and scavenges on dead animals and animal feces, it could carry pathogens. The bite itself can result in pain and swelling around the bite area, followed by headaches and nausea. Keep an eye on the wound for pus, as it could mean there is a secondary infection. And if there is swelling in the lymph nodes, seek medical attention.

This animal is almost entirely nocturnal, so it's unlikely you'll encounter it.

Preventing Giant Desert Centipede Bites

- Avoid reaching under rocks or other debris. There could be a centipede hiding there. Do not attempt to catch or handle a giant desert centipede.

Treatment of Bites

- Wash the wound with soap and warm water and carefully apply an antiseptic cream to prevent infection. Apply ice to reduce any swelling.

BOTTOM LINE

There is no need to worry about this intimidating-looking creature. The toxin it can deliver is not life threatening. You will likely not encounter them, as they are primarily nocturnal hunters. During the daytime they avoid the sun's heat by spending most of their time under rocks and debris. If you discover one, enjoy looking at it but leave it alone.

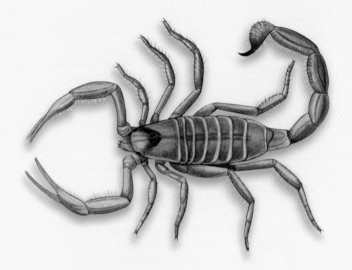

Scorpions

Scorpions have played a major role in the mythology of many different cultures. Serqet, the ancient Egyptian goddess of scorpions and venomous creatures, is often depicted wearing a headpiece in the shape of a scorpion, its characteristic stinger raised over its back. Several Greek legends involve the scorpion as well. In one, the great hunter Orion boasts that he could single-handedly hunt and kill every beast on earth. Artemis, the protector of life and the goddess of the hunt, enlisted the help of the scorpion to prove Orion wrong. The scorpion killed Orion with its venomous sting. In death, Orion was placed in the heavens, as was the scorpion (Scorpius), but Orion was placed far from Scorpius, and Scorpius chases Orion across the heavens; as one constellation rises, the other sets.

About Scorpions

Like ticks, chiggers and spiders, scorpions are arachnids. A scorpion's slender, extended body is segmented and equipped with 8 jointed legs. Its tail is segmented as well and arches over the scorpion's back, and the tail is tipped with a venomous stinger. Scorpions in the Southwest are less than 3 inches long.

Scorpions are efficient predators and prey upon small insects, spiders and even other scorpions. Despite their tough exoskeletons, scorpions are often prey themselves and are hunted by rodents, lizards, nocturnal birds (especially owls), bats and centipedes.

bark

striped-tailed

giant desert hairy

There are approximately 1,500 species of scorpions in the world, with 80 species in North America. It's estimated that 45 species inhabit the Southwest, but there is only 1 species to be concerned about—the bark scorpion.

The bark scorpion is easily recognized by its unstriped, straw-colored body and its very slender tail, which is only $^1/_{16}$ of an inch wide.

The most common species encountered in this region is the striped-tailed scorpion. Slightly smaller than the bark scorpion, the adults measure about $2^1/_2$ inches. The striped-tailed prefers burrowing in sandy soil but can be found in various habitats of the Southwest. Though it is venomous, it is not considered dangerous.

The largest, and arguably the most intimidating scorpion in the Southwest, is the giant desert hairy scorpion. This species is the largest scorpion in North America and full-grown specimens measure 5–7 inches in length.

On rare occasions, scorpions are accidentally transported in luggage or cargo and found outside of their natural range.

Life and Times . . .

A scorpion's front claws, called pedipalps, are important appendages for securing prey and for dancing, an important courtship ritual. Contrary to popular belief, the pedipalps are not legs.

During courtship, male and female scorpions locate each other by pheromones and vibration. Once they locate each other and determine that they are of the opposite sex, the male grabs the female's pedipalps with his own and drags her around in what looks like a frantic dance. He does this until he finds a place where he can deposit his spermatophore (a capsule containing a mass of his spermatozoa). The female draws the spermatophore into the underside of her abdomen and the sperm is released.

THINK TWICE

Think twice about reaching under any debris or items that might harbor a resting scorpion.

When camping, think twice about putting on shoes or clothing that have been lying on the ground. Be sure to inspect them first or they might harbor an unexpected guest.

Once the mating is complete, the male and female will go their own ways. The male is usually quick to leave, likely to avoid being cannibalized by the female, although sexual cannibalism is infrequent with scorpions.

The fertilized female will not give birth for several months, and in some species gestation requires more than a year. Scorpions are unusual among arthropods in that all species are viviparous—the young are born alive and look like miniature adults.

Unlike female ticks and spiders, which bear thousands of young, a female scorpion can bear 1–100 young, though the average litter size is 8. The young stay with the mother until after they shed their skin for the first time (molt); this usually occurs after about 2 weeks. Scorpions must molt several times before reaching sexual maturity; most species molt 5–7 times.

Scorpions are unusually long-lived compared to other invertebrates. In the wild, scorpions live 2–6 years, with females generally living longer than males.

Fascinating Facts

- Scorpions have remained essentially unchanged since they first appeared in oceans over 400 million years ago. Those early marine scorpions had external lungs. One recently discovered scorpion fossil was $8\frac{1}{2}$ feet long!

- Scorpions use highly sensitive hairs and slits on their legs to measure ground vibrations to determine the size and position of their next meal.

- Scorpions naturally fluoresce under long-wave ultraviolet light, and can be found in the dark by using a flashlight with an ultraviolet bulb or LED (a blacklight). Scorpions can be seen from many feet away as a green-colored glow. Using a UV flashlight is by far the best way to find scorpions.

Thanks to Scorpions

- Scorpion venom has medical applications; some venom contains compounds that alter the blood-clotting process, and research has shown that a synthetic version of a protein found in some venom can be used to treat brain cancer and tumors.

- In some countries, including Vietnam, scorpions are a specialty at restaurants and are used in making wine.

Myth Busters

MYTH: Scorpions will give you a painful pinch with their 2 claws.

While the front appendages look like nasty claws, they are called pedipalps. These pincerlike appendages are used to grasp prey, for defense and are used during mating. Bristles on the pedipalps help detect air currents and vibrations.

MYTH: Scorpions are so aggressive they sometimes sting themselves to death.

A scorpion's formidable tail and stinger arch over its back, sometimes so much so that the scorpion seems in danger of stinging itself, but this doesn't happen.

Why They Sting

Scorpions use their venomous stinger for defending themselves or for killing their prey. They do not aggressively pursue and sting large mammals.

How They Sting

At first glance, a scorpion looks a little like a crab, and its claws look like they could deliver a painful pinch. Nevertheless, the stinger, not the claws, are the scorpion's primary weapon.

A scorpion uses its large pincers to grab its prey; then, it arches its tail over its body and whips its tail downward, driving the stinger into the prey. Sometimes it stings repeatedly, and it can regulate how much of its venom it injects with each sting. If it uses all of its venom, it takes several days to replenish the supply. A scorpion's venom consists of various concentrations of nerve, blood and kidney toxins. Venom potency varies by species. Symptoms appear more quickly if venom enters the bloodstream rapidly or if a high concentration of venom is injected.

How Afraid Should I Be?

Scorpions are generally shy and not aggressive. They will sting humans only if threatened, cornered or disturbed. Accidental human stinging occurs when scorpions are touched while in their hiding places, with most stings occurring on the hands and feet.

Even in the unlikely event that you are stung, scorpion stings are not serious problems, as no scorpions found in the Southwest are particularly dangerous. The Arizona bark scorpion is the only potentially dangerous scorpion in the region. Even so, the last reported human death reported here was in 1948.

While a sting might cause a temporary burning pain, most are no worse than a honeybee sting and they are rarely, if ever, fatal. Young children and elderly people sometimes have more negative reactions to scorpion stings. Consequently, if they are stung, pay close attention for any serious symptoms.

Preventing Scorpion Stings

- Never touch a scorpion. Scorpions are best left alone.

- Remove any debris around your house or camp that might hide scorpions, and avoid probing barehanded under lumber, rocks or other places that might hide a scorpion. It is best to wear leather gloves, long pants and shoes when working around potential scorpion hideouts.

- Keep doors and windows of homes, tents and other shelters closed and caulk or repair any openings that scorpions might use to sneak in. Be sure to repair any torn screens and don't forget to check the dryer vent.

- When camping in scorpion country, be sure to shake out shoes, gloves and clothing before you put them on in the morning. Scorpions are nocturnal.

Thanks to Bats

- Bats are prolific insect eaters capable of devouring 600–1,000 mosquitoes an hour! Many of the bugs they eat are pests to humans.

- The southern and Mexican long-nosed bats are the only 2 nectar-feeding bats in this region and both are very important pollinators to native vegetation such as agave plants.

- The pallid bat, a common bat in the lower elevations of the Southwest, flies low to the ground in order to pick up the footsteps of their prey, which include beetles, crickets, centipedes, grasshoppers and even scorpions. These bats appear to be immune to the scorpions' venomous sting.

- Echolocation is remarkably similar to the active sonar used by modern antisubmarine systems. Active sonar systems emit short bursts of sound; these sound waves bounce off any objects in the area and are reflected back. Bats process these echoes subconsciously; submarines use complicated computer systems and talented sonar operators to determine location.

Myth Busters

MYTH: Bats are vicious carriers of rabies.

While some bats do transmit rabies, infected bats are rare—less than 1 percent of bats harbor the rabies virus.

MYTH: If you're not careful, a bat could get into your hair.

Not true. They certainly would not make a nest in the hair of such a dangerous creature. Thanks to echolocation, they can easily avoid foreign objects by swerving and weaving.

MYTH: Bats are filthy vermin!

While bat roosting areas often have a pile of dark, rice-sized droppings beneath them, the bats themselves always spend time cleaning and grooming themselves when they fly back to their roosts.

Why They Bite

When a bat feels threatened, its natural instinct is to flee or act defensively. The best defensive weapons they have are their tiny sharp teeth. While a bat bite is very rare, a bite by a rabid bat is even rarer.

How They Bite

As mammals, a bat's skeletal structure includes jaws and teeth. Bats have a unique pattern of teeth with a U-shaped gap separating the upper teeth; however, the dental equipment of these insect eaters is very small.

How Afraid Should I Be?

Get some sleep and don't worry about a bat biting you or your loved ones. Some fear that bats will suck the blood from your body. Thankfully, there are only 3 blood-eating bat species in the world and none of them live in the Southwest. You're far more likely to be in a car accident than be bitten by a rabid bat. In the United States, roughly 1 person dies each year from rabies due to a bat bite. Therefore, in a country with a population of approximately 300 million, your chances of being killed by a rabid bat are 1 in 300 million.

It's true that most of the human rabies cases in the Southwest and the United States are caused by rabies-infected bats. However, more than 99 percent of bats are rabies-free. Generally, bats infected with rabies die quickly.

THINK TWICE

Think twice about finding yourself in an attic or other close quarters where bat droppings have accumulated. There is a remote chance of becoming infected with histoplasmosis. This disease is contracted by inhaling spores of the fungus *Histoplasma capsulatum*. It can also be found in bird droppings.

The disease usually affects the lungs. Young children and older adults are particularly at risk. If untreated, the disease can be fatal. The best way to prevent it is to stay away from accumulations of bat or bird droppings. If you must frequent such an area, wear a respiratory mask.

Preventing Bat Bites

- Do not handle live bats with your bare hands. This is especially true for sick bats—don't mess with them!

- You can't get rabies by seeing a bat or touching its droppings, blood or urine. Touching a bat won't give you rabies unless the bat's saliva is

One of the most fascinating rattlesnake species in the region is the sidewinder. This snake prefers sandy deserts with sparse or no vegetation. The snake is named for the peculiar way it moves—a sideways movement over the sand. A common characteristic of the 3 subspecies of sidewinders is that they have elevated scales above their eyes that resemble horns. Biologists believe that these "horns" help protect the eyes from the sand.

sidewinder "horns"

Fascinating Facts

- Like all snakes, rattlesnakes shed their skin. They leave behind their skin by literally crawling out of the skin that covers the scales. This is called ecdysis. Each time they shed their skin they acquire a new button or rattle on their tail. They shed their skin up to 5 times their first summer; after that, they shed only 1–3 times per summer.

- The rattlesnake's loud, rapidly vibrating rattle is used to give a clear warning to anything seen as a threat to the snake.

- All rattlesnakes are viviparous. That means that they do not lay eggs; their young are born alive.

- The Southwest has more species of rattlesnakes (13) than any other region in the United States. Arizona tops the states in this region with 13 species. Even so, the likelihood of getting bitten by any of these is very, very remote.

- The U.S. Air Force dubbed its heat-seeking missiles "Sidewinders," which were named after the sidewinder rattlesnake.

- In 1776, Colonel Christopher Gadsden presented the Continental Congress with a flag depicting a rattlesnake and the slogan "Don't Tread On Me," a direct warning to the British that, like the rattlesnake, the colonists would defend themselves fiercely if necessary.

Thanks to Rattlesnakes

- Rattlesnake venom has anticoagulant properties, and potential medical applications of the venom have been extensively studied. The venom has been the subject of study for the treatment of arthritis, multiple sclerosis, strokes, heart attacks and polio.

- These snakes are quite beautiful and to see one (from a safe distance) is a thrilling and unforgettable experience.

- Rattlesnakes feed heavily on crop-damaging rodents. Plus, since snakes are members of a complex natural community, we have yet to discover all of their benefits.

Myth Busters

MYTH: All rattlesnake bites are venomous.

Approximately a quarter of all rattlesnake bites are dry bites, with no venom injected in the bite.

MYTH: Rattlesnakes will not strike in the dark.

Rattlesnakes can strike accurately in the dark. This is due to a pair of sensory pits located on both sides of the face, between the eye and the nostril. This characteristic is what lumps rattlesnakes into the group of snakes known as pit vipers. Keen heat-sensing cells located in the pit allow the snake to locate warm-blooded prey, day or night.

Why They Bite

Using toxic venom to kill prey is a brilliant survival strategy. The venom incapacitates the prey and the predatory snake can easily follow the dying creature and eat it without expending a lot of energy. The venom has a secondary benefit—for self-defense. Hence, the snake has venom for only two reasons: to secure food and to defend itself.

How They Bite

Any snake striking at you can be unnerving, but a rattlesnake bite is especially alarming. It happens in less than a second. Due to the fact that this is a venomous snake, it can kill you. But it is unlikely that it will.

The size of the rattlesnake, its age and health determine the potency and amount of venom that is delivered. Of the species covered here, the western diamondback rattlesnakes are the largest, most aggressive and most dangerous rattlesnakes.

A bite is nearly always preceded by rapid vibrating or rattling of the tail. This loud rattle serves as a clear warning to anything seen as a threat to the snake.

THINK TWICE

For the most part, snakes are quite secretive and will try to avoid human contact. Think twice about trying to catch a rattlesnake just to show you can do it. And think twice about killing the snake. They do not go around looking for people to bite.

Think twice about getting close to a rattling snake for a photo. Even coiled, they are capable of striking from about one-third of their body length away.

The bite itself is like a sudden, sharp, painful sting. The venom is injected by 2 specialized teeth called fangs. In some species, these teeth can measure nearly an inch long. The hollow canal inside the fang delivers the toxin from the venom supply to the tooth. The movable fangs resemble hypodermic needles and are capable of folding back in a sheath of membrane at the roof of the snake's mouth. When the snake strikes, the fangs extend forward to deliver the bite; even baby rattlesnakes have small fangs and are capable of injecting a small dose of venom. A snake sheds its fangs every 6–10 weeks.

The venom is a complex blend of chemical compounds. Many are proteins that are basically modified saliva enzymes, which begin the process of digesting prey even before the snake swallows it. The venom attacks the nervous system, particularly nerves that are critical for breathing and blood flow. It can also attack red blood cells and tissues, causing bruising and internal bleeding.

How Afraid Should I Be?

Approximately 5 people die of snakebites (from rattlesnakes and other venomous snakes) in the United States each year. Bee stings and dog bites result in more human deaths. Still, if you suddenly come upon a venomous

western diamondback

snake—or any snake for that matter—it might strike at you out of fear.

Though movies often depict encounters with writhing piles of snakes, snakes are generally solitary. Only during mating and hibernating periods do they occur in any numbers.

Metabolically, it is taxing for a snake to produce venom. Consequently, many snakes are thrifty in the use of their venom. Oftentimes the venomous

rattlesnake bite contains little or no venom; these so-called dry bites occur in roughly 25–50 percent of all rattlesnake bites.

Preventing Rattlesnake Bites

- Rattlesnake bites can penetrate lightweight shoes and clothing. If you know you will be in thick foliage, you might want to wear knee-high leather boots.

- Practice caution when inspecting piles of lumber or other items that might provide a hideout for rattlesnakes. Use care around outbuildings where rodents live, as these areas are good hunting grounds for snakes. Avoid rocky outcroppings, especially those facing south, where snakes might bask in the sun, particularly in early spring.

- If you see a rattlesnake, it will likely try to slither away. Be sure to give it a lane of escape. If it feels trapped, it will typically coil and buzz its tail. Move slowly away from any unusual buzzing sound.

- If you know you will be in an area where rattlesnake encounters are common, you might want to purchase a venom pump extractor, which suctions the venom from the area of the bite.

Myth Busters

MYTH: If in danger, a mother snake will swallow her young, spitting them out later once the danger has passed.

Parental care is not a very well-developed trait in snakes and there is certainly no evidence that mother snakes protect their young in this way. This myth may result from the fact that some snakes eat other smaller snakes, even those of their own species.

MYTH: All venomous snakes have triangular-shaped heads.

While some snakes do have triangular-shaped heads, coral snakes don't. And please note that many nonvenomous snakes have triangular-shaped heads, so this is not a good way to identify potentially venomous snakes.

THINK TWICE

Think twice about going barefoot outdoors at night. Western coral snakes mostly hunt at night.

Why They Bite

Using toxic venom to kill their prey is a brilliant survival strategy. The venom incapacitates the prey and the coral snake can easily follow the dying animal and eat it without expending a lot of unnecessary energy. The venom has a secondary benefit and that is for the snake's defense and well-being.

How They Bite

Rather than striking in a lightning-fast motion like a pit viper, coral snakes swing the forward portion of their body toward their prey until close enough to secure it. In order to release its venom, a coral snake chews with its short, unmovable fangs; this squeezes its venom glands, releasing the toxin. The bite itself is no more painful than being pricked by a needle. But once the venom reaches your central nervous system, it is very painful.

How Afraid Should I Be?

Its diminutive stature, small mouth and tiny fangs are all factors that minimize the real danger of this snake. Their small size also reduces the amount of venom that is released with a bite.

Less than 1 percent of snakebites reported in the United States are from coral snakes, and most of those bites were caused by people actually handling a coral snake.

What's more, coral snakes are nocturnal and quite secretive, making it very unlikely that you will be bitten.

Because the coral snake is a relative of the cobra, most folks believe its bite is nearly always fatal, but there have been no reported deaths caused by coral snake bites since coral snake antivenin became available. Statistics show that the bite of the coral snake is less threatening than a rattlesnake bite. Nevertheless, a coral snake bite requires immediate medical attention, as coral snake venom contains a neurotoxin that attacks the nervous system.

Preventing Coral Snake Bites

- The coral snake is primarily nocturnal, so don't wander around in the dark while barefoot.

- Be very cautious when poking around under piles of lumber, brush, logs, leaves and other debris.

- If you are fortunate enough to spy a coral snake, watch it from a distance. This way you will avoid being bitten and you won't stress the snake.

- Children are particularly attracted to the bright colors of the coral snake. Be sure to teach youngsters about this snake and other venomous snakes in your area. Please don't teach them that these snakes or other snakes are "bad"; instead, teach them respect for nature.

Treatment of Bites

- If someone is bitten, move them away from the snake and keep them calm.

- Lay the victim down, and position the bite slightly lower than the heart. Keep the victim as still as possible. Remove all rings, bracelets or watches from the limb of the bite. Wrap a snug, but not tight, elastic bandage around the bitten limb, just above the bite. This helps minimize the spread of the venom.

- Seek immediate medical help and get the victim to a medical facility as soon as possible. If possible, call ahead to warn medical personnel of a victim with a venomous snakebite. It is very helpful if you can identify the snake as a coral snake rather than a rattlesnake or other pit viper, as a specific antivenin exists for coral snakes.

- *Never* cut the snakebite, apply ice to the bite, suck the venom out with your mouth or give any drugs or alcohol to the victim. *Do not* apply a tourniquet to any venomous snakebite.

- If you are alone and must go for help, go slowly so as not to exert yourself. With prompt help, death is unlikely.

- The best snakebite kit includes a set of car keys, a cell phone and a companion.

BOTTOM LINE

This colorful snake is shy and is primarily nocturnal, so you're not likely to find one unless you start poking around under debris, logs and leaves. Be careful and avoid walking barefoot at night while outdoors in this region.

Other Snakes
Garter, Hognose, Gopher and Kingsnakes

As 12-year-olds, my buddy and I would flip over big pieces of scrap wood and sheet metal in hopes of finding a mess of garter snakes. When we saw one, we quickly grabbed it and stuffed it in a burlap sack. Of course, we occasionally got bitten. What would you do if some screeching giant pounced on you?

Worse yet, we'd take the writhing sack home to proudly show our catch to other family members—who we knew would get creeped out. We thought it was cool, but we were too young to know that we were reinforcing the universal fear and hatred for this innocent group of animals.

About These Snakes

There are roughly 140 species of snakes in United States and Canada. In the Southwest, Arizona alone is home to more snake species than any other state—42 species of nonvenomous snakes and 12 species of venomous snakes. In the Southwest, most snake species, venomous or not, will bite or threaten to bite you if you threaten or mishandle them.

For brevity's sake I will briefly cover 4 common nonvenomous snakes found in the Southwest: garter snakes, hognose snakes (sometimes called blow snakes), gopher snakes and kingsnakes.

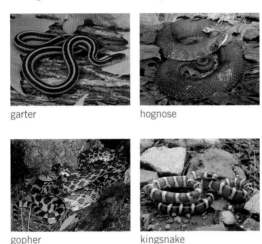

garter   hognose

gopher   kingsnake

Life and Times . . .

COMMON GARTER SNAKE

This is the most common and widespread snake in North America; in this region there are 5 subspecies. Most are easily recognized by the 3 yellow-to-cream stripes that run the length of the body. The background color of the snake is black or grayish brown. Rather than live in rocky, dry areas, garter snakes prefer living within a reasonable distance of water or wet areas.

Garter snakes will bite if confronted or captured. They thrash wildly when caught and often release their feces and a foul-smelling, musky spray that is potent and not easy to wash off.

western hognose snake playing dead

WESTERN HOGNOSE SNAKES

The western hognose snake is the most frightening-looking non-poisonous snake in our region; when it is threatened, it flattens out its head like a cobra, hisses loudly and often strikes . . . with a closed mouth.

A stout-bodied snake, the western hognose is lightly colored, usually tan or buffy gray. Its common name comes from its pronounced upturned, hoglike nose that they use to burrow after prey. If its seemingly aggressive behavior doesn't send you down the trail, it will roll on its back, open its mouth, hang its tongue out and do a fantastic job of playing dead. Its hope is that if it looks dead, you will leave it alone. Like the garter snake, it also has the ability to discharge a foul-smelling substance that might urge you to leave it alone.

GREAT BASIN GOPHER SNAKES

This is the longest snake in the Southwest. Adults can measure up to 7 feet long! (The average size is around 4 feet in length.) The gopher snake's back is covered with dark brown blotches on a background color of yellow, tan or cream. A dark stripe on the head runs from the front of the eye to the angle of the jaw.

This open-country snake spends much of its time in semi-brushy areas, where it hunts underground burrowing mammals such as mice and gophers. It will also feed on some birds and bird eggs. Because it often hunts underground, it is not encountered very often.

When confronting a person, the snake will likely coil, buzz its tail and hiss very loudly. Because of this behavior, and because its coloration resembles that of a rattlesnake, it is often confused for a venomous snake and is unfortunately often killed by humans. A large adult gopher snake can deliver a painful bite if threatened.

KINGSNAKES

This medium-sized, widespread snake is ringed in colorful bands and is sometimes confused with the venomous western coral snake where their ranges overlap. But remember, on a coral snake red touches yellow; on a kingsnake, red touches black. There are several subspecies such as the Utah mountain and Arizona mountain kingsnakes. This group of snakes prefers riparian areas and is encountered less often in open and arid desert areas.

This ground-dwelling snake is a powerful constrictor that feeds on small mammals, birds, lizards and oftentimes on other snakes, including rattlesnakes! They seem to be immune to the venom from a rattlesnake bite.

Arizona mountain kingsnake

Fascinating Facts

- The common toad has a pair of glands on the back of its neck that can discharge a poison that makes it distasteful to most animals. The western hognose snake must think the poison is delicious; it loves eating toads!

- A breastbone called the sternum connects our ribs. Snakes do not have sternums. They have floating ribs, which allow them to move in a side-to-side motion and to swallow items larger than their own heads.

Thanks to Snakes

- They often feed on insects and small rodents that can be harmful to agricultural crops, and all snakes play an important role in the natural environment by contributing to ecological systems as predators and prey.

Myth Busters

MYTH: A snake's tongue is poisonous!

Not true. The tongue is a sensory organ used to detect smells. It picks up scent molecules and brushes them across a special organ on the roof of the mouth called a Jacobson's organ.

MYTH: Snakes are slimy!

This is a common misconception. Snakes are sometimes confused with amphibians, which have moist, slimy skin; at first glance, a snake's scales (and particularly the larger belly scales) are smooth and often shiny, making them appear wet. In reality, snakes and other reptiles have small dry scales.

Why They Bite

All of the snakes mentioned above will always try their best to avoid confrontations with humans. Flight and camouflage are their primary means of escape. However, if captured or cornered they often strike and bite.

How They Bite

None of these snakes have sharp fangs. Though their recurved teeth are sharp, they are quite small.

How Afraid Should I Be?

No need to be afraid. None of these snakes are venomous, and none have large teeth. Some of the larger snakes might break your skin with a bite, but the wound will be shallow and may not even bleed. With that said, if you or other family members handle reptiles, be aware that nearly all reptiles carry *Salmonella* bacteria and they often shed these bacteria in their feces. While these bacteria don't cause illness in snakes, *Salmonella* can cause serious illness in people. Most exposure results in diarrhea, fever and abdominal cramps. However, if it spreads to the bloodstream, bone marrow or nervous system, the infection can be serious and sometimes fatal. For the bacteria to spread to humans, fingers or objects that have been contaminated with reptile feces must be placed in the mouth. Thankfully, preventing *Salmonella* infection is easy. *Always* wash your hands with hot, soapy water after handling reptiles (snakes, lizards and turtles).

Preventing Snake Bites

- Don't crowd a snake. If you threaten it, it might bite.

Treatment of Bites

- It's okay to let out a "Yikes!"—but that is usually all you will have to do.

- If the bite breaks your skin, wash the wound and cover with a bandage if necessary. Watch it for the next few days for a secondary infection.

THINK TWICE

Think twice about picking up a snake. Unless you catch it properly and handle it gently, you might be bitten.

BOTTOM LINE

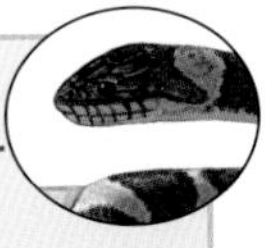

There is no need to be afraid. Snakes will do everything in their power to avoid you, and a bite from an undisturbed snake is very rare. Even if you manage to accidentally corner or upset one, these snakes are not venomous and don't have large teeth.

Skunks

It was mid-March and as we were driving back to Aunt Angeline's farm one evening, we had our car windows open a crack. In the darkness we came to a point where the unmistakable smell of the first skunk of the spring wafted into the car. Aunt Angeline inhaled deeply, and with great satisfaction she declared, "Ahh, there's nothing like a two-toned kitty with fluid drive!"

About Skunks

The Southwest is home to 4 species of skunks. While striped skunks and the smaller western spotted skunks can be found across the whole region, common hog-nosed skunks and hooded skunks are more limited in their range.

striped

western spotted

hog-nosed

hooded

STRIPED SKUNKS

Striped skunks, also known as polecats, are easily the most common skunk species in the region. These house cat-sized skunks have a "V" stripe that meets at the base of its head.

WESTERN SPOTTED SKUNKS

Western spotted skunks, sometimes called civet cats or weasel skunks, are the smallest skunks of the group. Unrelated to cats, they weigh 1–3 pounds. They are more agile and quick than the other regional skunks. They have a white spot on the forehead and the various stripes that run along their back resemble spots. Their banded tail is only 6–8 inches long.

HOG-NOSED SKUNKS

Common hog-nosed skunks, found in the Southwest only in Arizona and New Mexico, have a solid white stripe, a white tail and no white on the top of the head. These are also called rooter skunks because of their habit of rooting up insects and grubs with their broad, slightly upturned nose pad.

Hog-nosed skunks prefer rocky areas for denning sites. Not only do they winter in such dens, but they also use them as nurseries. Unlike the striped skunk, this species is more or less unsocial.

HOODED SKUNKS

Hooded skunks are mostly white from the top of their head to the tip of their tail. Their legs, underbelly and bottom of the tail are black. The ruff of long white hair that often forms at the back of the neck resembles a hood and is the origin of their common name. They have a very limited range in North America, but they are found in southeastern Arizona and southwestern New Mexico. Rarely seen because of their nocturnal manner, these skunks prefer riparian areas (areas located on the bank of a waterway).

Life and Times . . .

If you want attention, make noise or dress wildly. In a world where most animals wear subdued colors so that they might better blend in with the countryside, skunks do not follow the rules. Their message is a loud and clear "HEY, LOOK AT ME! HERE I AM!"

These distinctly striped, black-and-white, cat-sized mammals are primarily nocturnal, so we rarely encounter them. When we do, it is usually in spring, summer and fall. During the winter months, many skunks in colder regions live in a den, sometimes sharing one with up to a dozen skunks. Such cuddling helps conserve energy.

Unlike their northerly kin, skunks living in the more moderate portions of the Southwest can be active in the winter.

Skunks are most commonly found in farmland or semi-open areas. They tend to avoid forests. Active at night, they den up during the day in old woodchuck and badger burrows, and underneath rock piles,

striped skunk

hollow trees or outbuildings. I remember discovering a skunk when a boyhood buddy and I flipped over an old car hood lying on the ground. We were looking for snakes but discovered a startled skunk!

hog-nosed skunk

All skunks are capable of delayed implantation—after mating, the fertilized egg remains dormant for months before it is implanted in the uterine wall and development of the embryo continues. For this reason, mating of the western spotted skunk often occurs in September or October, with implantation delayed until March. This is the only time of the year when adult males and females are found together.

The female gives birth to 4–7 babies (kittens) from April to early June. The kittens stay with their mother for up to a year, though kittens are capable of breeding after 10 months.

Skunks are omnivores, feeding both on plants and animals. Like raccoons, they are quite opportunistic. They will feed on human garbage, bird eggs and even carrion. Since they often eat beetle grubs, ants and other underground insects, their front claws—longer than the back claws—are perfect tools for digging. Skunk diggings are common signs of their whereabouts.

Fascinating Facts

- Scientists long considered skunks a member of the weasel family (Mustelidae), but in 1997, a group of taxonomists determined that skunks were genetically very different from other Mustelidae members. For this reason, North American skunks and the related Asian stink badgers were put into their own separate weasel family called Mephitidae.

- Skunks have enough smelly liquid for 5 sprays. After that, it takes 10 days or so to produce more.

- The English word "skunk" is derived from the Algonquian Indian word *seganku*, meaning "one who squirts."

Thanks to Skunks

- Skunks, and especially young skunks, are prey for great horned owls, foxes, coyotes and bobcats.

- Skunks are an important component of the rich biodiversity of the Southwest.

Myth Busters

MYTH: If your dog gets sprayed, give it a bath in tomato juice.

This old wives' tale has been around for some time. What really happens is that when your nose is subjected to a high dose of skunk spray, you develop what is called olfactory fatigue. This means that your nose quits smelling the odor. Instead, you can easily smell the tomato juice and convince yourself that the skunk smell has been washed away, but someone coming upon the scene will gasp and tell you that the skunk smell is awful.

western spotted skunk

Why They Bite or Spray

When a skunk feels threatened, it will either lope away or lift its tail straight up, with all the tail hair erect to make the tail as noticeable as possible. The message is "Watch it! Don't bother me!" A skunk also possesses 2 other defensive weapons—sharp teeth and a strong bite. While a skunk bite is very rare, a bite by a rabid skunk is even more uncommon.

How They Bite (and Spray!)

Like other carnivorous mammals, skunks have 4 sharp canine teeth and scissorlike premolars called carnassials (last upper premolars and first lower molars). These teeth are adaptations dedicated to killing prey, and used to cut and tear meat. Clearly these same tools can be used as defensive weapons, and they are capable of delivering a nasty bite.

With such short, stubby legs, it isn't easy for a skunk to outrun a predator. The striped skunk has developed a unique defense system. When a skunk is threatened, it first tries to run away from the predator. If that doesn't work, it tries to frighten the attacker by arching its back, raising its tail and turning its back toward the threat. It may also stomp its feet. If this doesn't work, as a last resort, the skunk will spray the animal with a strong-smelling fluid. The fluid really stinks and can also sting the predator's eyes—giving the skunk time to get away. A skunk can spray as far as 15 feet!

Before spraying, the smaller spotted skunk will perform a comical-looking series of handstands while facing the intruder and fire directly over its own head.

How Afraid Should I Be?

It is highly unlikely that you or your family will be faced with a skunk bite. A potentially dangerous skunk is one that becomes unafraid of humans. Normally these are shy, nonaggressive animals.

You should be suspicious of any skunk that is:

- acting unusually, boldly or aggressively
- moving about during daylight hours
- walking irregularly, almost as if it were drunk

If it displays one of these symptoms, there is a slight chance that it has rabies.

Non-Bite Concerns

Far and away the greatest fear in dealing with skunks is their chemical warfare weaponry. Being sprayed, or even being in the vicinity of a skunk spraying, is truly an unforgettable experience. Of course, the skunk is hoping that you will not forget it and perhaps next time you will give it a wide berth!

THINK TWICE

Think twice about moving in to get the perfect photo of a skunk. If necessary, the skunk can spray its noxious delivery up to 15 feet!

Think twice when observing any skunk that is acting uncharacteristically bold. It could be harboring a disease or the rabies virus.

striped skunk

If a skunk sprays you, it can cause nausea and cause your eyes to burn. At the very least, you will likely find the encounter aromatically unpleasant!

The skunk's spray is a yellow oil composed of chemical compounds, called thiols, which contain sulfur. The foul concoction is stored in 2 prune-sized glands with openings in the skunk's anus.

Prior to spraying, the skunk will turn its rear end to face the threat (you!) and lift its plumelike tail straight up. The message at this point is a very clear "Okay, this is a warning! Back off!"

Preventing Skunk Bites or Sprays

- The best advice is to simply steer clear of wild skunks. Do not feed them or try to approach them. And if one tries to approach you or you see one with its tail standing, move away!

Treatment of Bites and Sprays

- Treat a skunk bite as you would a cat or dog bite. If the wound is severe, seek medical attention. Since skunks are wild animals, you should contact the proper animal control agency and your doctor or the department of health for further advice. The offending animal should be tested for the rabies virus after biting a human.

- If you have been sprayed by a skunk, take off your clothes outside your home to prevent it from being "skunked." To remove skunk odor from your clothes or cleanup towels, wash them with 1 cup of liquid laundry bleach per gallon of water.

- Take a very long, soapy shower!

- If your dog or cat has been sprayed, bathe the animal in a mixture of 1 quart of 3 percent hydrogen peroxide (purchase at a drugstore), ¼ cup of baking soda (sodium bicarbonate) and 1 teaspoon of liquid detergent. After 5 minutes of bathing, rinse your pet with water and repeat bathing if necessary. Be careful to keep the solution out of the pet's eyes and mouth. To be effective, the mixture must be fresh, not stored. Note that the mixture might temporarily bleach your pet's hair.

- Products, such as Skunk-Off, are available for deodorizing pets. Carefully follow the directions, and keep in mind that none of these remedies work as well as time. Over the course of 2–3 weeks, the compounds in the spray will break down on their own.

BOTTOM LINE

It's highly unlikely that you or your family will be bitten by a skunk. Normally these are shy, nonaggressive animals. You are much more likely to be sprayed. While unpleasant, this is also a rare occurrence as long as you give skunks a wide berth—especially if one raises its tail!

Turtles
Snapping Turtles and Spiny Softshell Turtles

Snapping turtles have an image problem. Even their name, "snapping turtle," indicates aggressiveness. They are not cute. In fact, they are quite homely and their nature is one of a grumpy old man. As youngsters, my friends and I used to spend summers swimming in an abandoned gravel pit. A rarely seen, giant snapping turtle we called "Old Moses" lived at the pit. This snapper became a legend and more than once while swimming, one of my buddies would scream out, "It's Old Moses! I felt him with my foot!!" Like junior Olympians we would race out of the water to the security of dry land, where we would catch our breath glad that we had escaped with all of our toes. Little did we know that unprovoked snappers will not bite toes while in the water.

About Turtles

Turtles have managed to survive on earth much longer than humans, and over millions of years they've adapted to live in almost any freshwater aquatic habitat. In the Southwest they are mostly found along large rivers and other slow-moving bodies of water. Two potentially aggressive turtle species—snapping turtles and spiny softshell turtles—live in the region.

common snapping

spiny softshell

Snapping turtles are significantly larger than other turtles in the Southwest. In this region, 30–40 pound snappers are not uncommon and giant specimens can weigh 50 pounds.

Snappers are omnivores and eat both plant and animal material. Excellent scavengers and stealthy hunters, they hunt by sitting still on the bottom of the wetland and ambushing prey.

The Southwest is home to another potentially aggressive turtle species—the spiny softshell turtle. More aquatic in nature than the snapping turtle, this reptile is native only to the eastern part of the region but has been introduced in other parts of the region. The only native subspecies is the Texas Spiny Softshell. All softshell turtles are easily recognized by their rubbery, smooth shell and long, piglike nose; these turtles are shy and uncommonly encountered. Like snapping turtles, softshelled turtles are occasionally hooked by anglers. When frightened (e.g., when they are being pulled into a boat), they will likely will try to bite. In such instances, it's often best to free the turtle by simply cutting the line.

Life and Times . . .

Snapping turtles mate at about 5 years of age. Once mating has occurred, the female snapping turtle heads to land and digs a hole with one of her back legs

common snapping turtle hatchling

before depositing 25–50 round white eggs. This typically occurs in May or June. She covers the eggs with soil before leaving. The warmth of the sun on the soil incubates them.

In roughly $2^{1}/_{2}$ months, the eggs hatch and the hatchling turtles must dig their way out of the nest. However, during cool summers, the eggs might remain in the ground and hatch the following spring. The hatchlings are never more vulnerable in their life than when they must make the dangerous (and often lengthy) journey from their birth nest to water.

The pugnacious softshell turtle has evolved for an aquatic lifestyle. Its flattened profile allows it to swim and walk easily in a river's current and hide, buried in a sandy river bottom. Its long neck allows it to periodically reach the surface to project its elongated snout, like a snorkel, to take a breath of air. When buried, the camouflaged turtle hunts by ambushing passing crayfish, tadpoles, small fish, and invertebrates.

Even though this turtle spends some time basking in the sunshine, it is always quick to take to the water, even if only mildly disturbed. They are clearly not comfortable on land, and this is evident when the female lays eggs. When seeking a sandy shoreline for egg laying, the female rarely goes more than 1 00 yards from water before aggressively digging a nest in which to lay her 15–38 eggs.

Fascinating Facts

- Since these turtles spend so much time in the water, their shells are often covered in green algae. Other species, such as painted turtles, bask in the sun more often, making it difficult for algae to grow.

- As with other turtle species, the temperature of the soil covering the buried eggs determines the sex of snapping turtles. Warmer soil temperatures tend to produce females.

- Snappers are capable of living for decades, much longer than most animals. The average lifespan of a snapping turtle is an estimated 30–40 years.

Thanks to Turtles

- Turtles are important members of the cleanup crew in aquatic communities. Falsely accused of having a negative effect on fish populations, they actually help keep fisheries healthy by feeding on sick, injured or dead fish. It is extremely difficult for them to catch a healthy fish.

- Turtle eggs and hatchlings are often prey for raccoons, skunks, foxes, coyotes, herons and other predators.

Myth Busters

MYTH: The snapping turtle will bite off your finger or toe if it grabs you!

Though they make a lunging snap and an audible hiss, it is unlikely that one will sever any of your digits. Nevertheless, the larger the turtle and the more you struggle, the more likely you are to experience an open wound.

MYTH: During hibernation, snapping turtles can hold their breath all winter.

Snapping turtles and softshell turtles overwinter in hibernation on the bottom of wetlands. Without oxygen, they would die. They survive by slowing their metabolism to the point where their biological systems are barely functioning. This requires very little oxygen, and they are able to absorb the little oxygen they need from the water itself. Most pond and lake water contains dissolved oxygen. The dissolved oxygen is absorbed directly through the turtle's thin skin, which is

common snapping turtle

rich in a network of blood capillaries, found inside its mouth and around its rear end.

Why They Bite

Snapping turtles and softshell turtles only bite when they feel threatened. Most bites occur when the turtle is out of the water.

How They Bite

As with other turtles, these reptiles have no teeth. Instead, a turtle's mouth resembles a beak. Its sharp edges cut and shear food items ranging from crayfish and fish to salamanders, snails and plants. Therefore a turtle bite is capable of cutting you. To defend itself, a snapping turtle will turn to face its attacker; be forewarned, it can extend its neck half the length of its upper shell!

How Afraid Should I Be?

Turtles are animals with reputations bigger than their bite. In reality, these primitive reptiles are not anywhere near the threat they are perceived to be. Turtle bites are extremely rare and they rarely happen in the water. However, a bite is likely on land—if you put yourself too close to the mouth of a frightened turtle. And the bite is simply a fear-based response; in reality, we are a threat to turtles, not the other way around.

Preventing Turtle Bites

- You can swim worry-free because they will *not* bite you in the water unless you are very careless and pose a threat to them. They will *not* pursue swimmers.

- When you encounter a turtle out of the water, simply keep your distance and do not harass the turtle with sticks or other objects. Annoyed turtles are more likely to bite in their own defense.

common snapping turtle

Treatment of Bites

- If a turtle bites you and holds on, do not attempt to pull away. It will let go on its own. Admittedly, your first response is to pull away, but if you do, you increase the risk of the bite cutting you.

- Instead, try to stay calm, grit your teeth and patiently wait for the turtle to release its grip.

- If you receive a cut, wash it with clean water and soap, bandage it and seek medical attention if necessary.

BOTTOM LINE

Turtles are nowhere near the threat people perceive them to be. Bites are extremely rare and only happen when a turtle feels threatened. Enjoy sightings of this prehistoric-looking animal from a respectful distance, and do not put yourself anywhere near its mouth. A snapping turtle can, and will, extend its neck half the length of its shell to defend itself.

Raccoons

"There is a beast they call aroughcun ["he who scratches with his hands"], much like a badger, but useth to live [in] trees as squirrels do. Their squirrels some are near as great as our smallest sort of wild rabbits, some blackish or black and white, but the most are gray."

—Captain John Smith, author of *Generall Historie of Virginia* (1624)

About Raccoons

There are more raccoons in the Southwest today than there were 200 years ago. This adaptable mammal—which is famous for the distinctive black mask over its eyes, and its fluffy, black-ringed tail—is both loved and scorned. Like a bandit, it can steal your heart, or your picnic.

Though its long, sharp canine teeth clearly lump it into the mammalian order Carnivora, the raccoon is an omnivore that eats a broad range of foods and will not pass up an opportunity to fill its belly.

Its keen hearing, excellent night vision and amazing sense of touch are all adaptations for the nightlife it favors over daytime adventures.

Life and Times . . .

Raccoons prefer to live near trees and water. Though more common in stands of deciduous trees than in coniferous forests, this highly adaptable animal is comfortable living in both urban and wild environments. It is not unusual to find raccoons in abandoned houses or barns.

One reason this opportunistic mammal is so widespread is that it can eat a wide range of foods. An omnivore, it eats fruit, nuts, seeds, garden crops, such as corn and watermelons, as well as insects, bird eggs, crayfish, fish, frogs, small rodents, human trash and carrion (particularly roadkill).

In the Southwest, male raccoons are slightly larger than females and begin to look for a mate in February, with mating peaking in March. Raccoons are capable of breeding all spring and into summer. After roughly 65 days of pregnancy, the female gives birth to 2–6 young.

After a month or so, the young leave their birthing den and join the mother in foraging for food. They will stay with their mother through their first winter before heading out on their own the following spring. One-year-old females are capable of breeding and producing young.

Raccoons are said to "hibernate" during periods of inclement weather. Not true hibernators, they do become dormant at chillier elevations and will often share denning quarters. This cuddling behavior conserves heat and helps them survive cold weather.

Fascinating Facts

- Related to coatis and ringtails, the raccoon is the only member of the Procyonidae family found in the Southwest region. (*Procyon* is Latin for "before dogs." This refers to the fact that the raccoon's ancestors have been around longer than those of dogs and wolves.)

- Some American Indians refer to the raccoon as the "bear's little brother." Like a bear, it walks on all 4 feet with an arch in its back and has claws that don't retract. And like humans and bears, the raccoon walks using the entire sole of the foot "heel to toe."

- Their clawed feet, each bearing 5 toes, help make them excellent tree climbers. Their reasonably long tail serves as an aid in balance.

Thanks to Raccoons

- Raccoon fur has been harvested for clothing for centuries.

- Raccoons are a food item for other wildlife such as coyotes. They are also a food source for some people.

- They are an important component to the rich biodiversity of the Southwest.

Myth Busters

MYTH: Raccoons always wash their food before eating it.

While this might be good advice for us, it is not the case with raccoons. Their species name *lotor* means "washer," but raccoons do not always dunk their food, even when near water, and will not hesitate to eat when water is not nearby. Biologists are unsure as to why raccoons have this strange habit.

Why They Bite

When threatened, the raccoon's natural instinct is to flee or act defensively. Its best defensive weapons are its sharp teeth and strong bite. While a raccoon bite is very rare, a bite by a rabid raccoon is even rarer.

How They Bite

Like other carnivorous mammals, raccoons have 4 sharp canine teeth and scissorlike shearing premolars called carnassial teeth (last upper premolars and first lower molars). These are adaptations for killing prey, and for cutting and tearing meat. Clearly they can also be used as defensive weapons. Given the raccoon's speed, its relatively strong jaws and sharp teeth, it is capable of delivering a nasty bite.

THINK TWICE

Think twice about keeping a baby raccoon for a pet. In fact, it may be illegal for you to keep one as a pet without a proper permit.

Think twice about feeding a raccoon. Putting your hand in front of any wild animal's mouth is never a good idea. A seemingly harmless situation could turn into a bite delivered by the nervous raccoon.

How Afraid Should I Be?

It is unlikely that you or a member of your family will be bitten by a raccoon. A potentially dangerous raccoon is one that becomes unafraid of humans. Normally these are shy, nonaggressive animals. You should be suspicious of any raccoon that is acting boldly or aggressively. There is a slight chance that it is infected with rabies.

Non-Bite Concerns

RABIES

Only mammals are affected by the rabies virus, which is carried in saliva. Rabies is a serious infection of the nervous system. If not treated quickly, it is capable of making a person very ill and death almost always results.

Rabies is occasionally found in raccoons. In the United States, more than 7,000 animals (wild and domestic) are diagnosed with rabies annually. It is usually transmitted by a bite. Though non-bite infections are rare, it is possible for infected saliva to enter the eyes, nose, mouth, or an open wound.

Avoid contact with any raccoon that displays unusual, bold or sickly behavior. Animals that have rabies are often described as "foaming at the mouth." This happens because the animal's nerves no longer work properly and it can't swallow its own saliva. If you find a dead raccoon, do not handle it with bare hands. For more on rabies, see pp. 10–11.

RACCOON ROUNDWORM (*BAYLISASCARIS PROCYONIS*)

Though it is not the result of a bite, a roundworm found in the feces of some raccoons can cause misery in humans. Raccoons are the primary host of this roundworm, which is commonly found in their small intestines. If it infects a human, the microscopic, migrating roundworms can cause skin irritations, as well as eye and brain damage. There have only been a handful of human deaths, all of them in children, but one should be aware of the possibility of transmission nonetheless.

Raccoon feces can carry millions of roundworm eggs. Humans can encounter the eggs through contact with raccoon droppings or by touching a contaminated area or object (the eggs persist long after the feces disappear). Small children are especially vulnerable because they often put their fingers, objects or even droppings into their mouth. Any area contaminated with raccoon feces should be cleaned and the feces should be burned, along with any affected feed, straw, hay or other materials. Raccoons are also hosts for leptospirosis and giardiasis, both of which can be a health concern for humans.

Preventing Raccoon Bites and Roundworm

- The best advice is to not approach wild raccoons or allow them to approach you.

- The best way to prevent a roundworm infection is to minimize contact with any area inhabited by raccoons. Roundworm eggs are very resistant to environmental conditions and can survive for several years. Children and pets should be kept away from these contaminated areas until a thorough cleaning has occurred. It is important to keep decks and picnicking areas around your home clean of food scraps, as these might attract raccoons. Carefully pouring boiling water over the surface where droppings were left is one way to minimize contact with the parasite eggs.

Treatment of Bites and Roundworm

- Treat a raccoon bite as you would a cat or dog bite. Wash the wound, stop the bleeding with a compress, bandage it and seek medical attention. Since raccoons are wild animals, you should contact the proper animal control agency and your doctor or the department of health for further advice.

- Puncture wounds should be thoroughly flushed and cleaned with a topical antibiotic. Deep puncture wounds require medical assistance.

- After receiving medical care, monitor the bite for a possible infection.

- Rabies is treatable through a series of vaccinations. Every year approximately 40,000 people in the United States receive these shots as a precaution.

- Roundworm treatment is very difficult. If someone's been exposed, or even suspects exposure to raccoon roundworm, seek immediate medical care. There are currently no drugs that can effectively kill the larvae moving in the body. Laser surgery has been successfully performed to kill larvae present in the retina of the eye, but the damage caused by the migrating larvae is irreversible. Treatment with steroids in intermediate hosts is mainly supportive and is designed to decrease the inflammatory reaction.

- Getting a tetanus shot is a good idea.

BOTTOM LINE

It's unlikely that you or a member of your family will be bitten by a raccoon. Still, a raccoon that is sick, injured or has become unafraid of humans is a potentially dangerous animal. Reduce your risk by not approaching raccoons or allowing them to approach you—especially ones that are acting boldly or aggressively.

Collared Peccaries
or Javelinas

For those who have read *Old Yeller*, you might recall the chilling account of the wild hogs tearing into Old Yeller as he keeps the sharp-tusked pigs from getting to his master, Travis. The author of this children's classic tale does not make it clear if the threatening animals are feral hogs or javelinas. It doesn't really matter because the image is terrifying. In reality, peccaries are very shy and will go out of their way to avoid an encounter with a human. And for a real dose of reality, consider this: the javelina only resembles a pig—they are not members of the swine family at all!

About Collared Peccaries or Javelinas

In the Southwest, collared peccaries (also called javelinas) are most common in the arid, mesquite habitats of New Mexico, Arizona and Nevada. There are no records of wild populations of javelina (pronounced hah-vuh-lee-na) in southern California and Utah. The highly gregarious collared peccary earns its name for the white band of coarse hair around its neck. The rest of its body is covered in grizzled black and gray coarse hairs, with a pronounced ridge of hairs that run from the head to the rump. This desert dweller is an expert in surviving and thriving in the dry, shrubby, rocky washes of the Southwest. Ranging in groups, they forage for their favorite foods, prickly pear cacti and agave; both species are also a good source of water. They also feed on roots, insects and even bird eggs. They usually live near a watering hole or some other water source. While they have poor eyesight, their sense of hearing is good and their sense of smell is excellent. By herding together they combine these sensory skills in order to avoid becoming prey to cougars, coyotes and human hunters.

Life and Times . . .

An adult male javelina can weigh 50–55 pounds, while an adult female will be slightly smaller. They stand 18–24 inches at the shoulder and have very slender legs and small 3-toed hooves; pigs have 4. The well-developed canine teeth, often referred to as tusks, are excellent tools for defense and fighting other javelinas, particularly among males fighting for dominance.

The social unit is a band of 10–20 animals that is comprised of all age groups. A dominant male does all the breeding and will breed at any time of the year. The social hierarchy revolves around the dominant male followed by the rest of the javelinas from largest to smallest.

After mating, the gestation period is roughly 145 days. When conditions are good, particularly if the season has been rainy, the birth rate is higher. Baby javelinas are known as reds because of their red color. Javelinas have a very high reproductive potential as they are capable of having 2 litters per year.

A birthing female will separate herself from the band, seeking a den or hollow log where she gives birth to 1–3 young. Within a day or so she will rejoin the band with her young. She is very defensive around her young, as others in the band might try to kill and eat the reds. Only the birth mother's sisters are tolerated and they often play the role of nursemaid and help raise the young. The young are weaned after 2–3 months and then become part of the band, sleeping, foraging and eating together.

Fascinating Facts

- The origin of the word "javelina" is from the Spanish word *jabalina*, which means "javelin."

- Javelinas are the only wild ungulate (hoofed mammal) in the western hemisphere with a year-long breeding season. Other ungulates, such as deer or antelope, have a defined breeding period when the female comes into estrus.

- Unlike pigs, javelinas have a musk gland back near their rump. Consequently, some call this wild animal the musk hog. While humans find the smell offensive, the javelinas become familiar with each individual's fragrance and they can easily keep track of their band. They will also rub against rocks, trees or brush as a means of scent marking to make their territory known to other javelinas. In javelina country you can often smell them before you see them.

Thanks to Collared Peccaries or Javelinas

- Peccaries provide hunting opportunities and wild game for thousands of resident and nonresident hunters in the Southwest.

- Scores of plant species are dispersed by peccaries. Peccaries unknowingly engineer the landscape by feeding on many species of plants.

- Products made from peccary leather, such as boots, shoes and gloves, are revered by sporting clientele in Europe.

Myth Busters

MYTH: Javelinas are closely related to pigs.

The javelina is a peccary, not a pig. While it resembles a pig in body shape and form and has a flexible, piglike snout, it has only 6–9 tail vertebrae; a pig has 20–23. Peccaries have slim legs with tiny hooves and are more closely related to the tapir—a tropical mammal found in Central and South America.

MYTH: Javelinas are really vicious.

On the contrary, they will readily flee. Their poor eyesight sometimes brings a fleeing javelina very close to you and it might wrongly be interpreted as a charge. They may defend their young if your dog is present; this is because they have a natural hatred of coyotes, one of the javelina's natural predators.

Why They Bite

The only reason they bite is in defense of their small herd, particularly their young. Javelinas hate coyotes and therefore, by association, they dislike dogs. There have been cases of humans getting in the way of an angry herd of javelinas that suddenly (and often chaotically) go after a dog. If the dog retreats to the owner, mistaken bites could result. Overall, javelinas avoid humans and will usually quickly retreat.

THINK TWICE

Think twice about reaching out to pet a little baby javelina. While a band of javelinas might forage near your home, appear docile and might even get used to your presence, they are wild animals and the mother might consider you a threat.

Think twice about letting your dog roam freely on a hike while strolling through javelina habitat such as rocky washes. Javelinas do not like coyotes and your dog is a close enough relative to the coyote that javelinas consider them the enemy. Your dog could be attacked, seriously injured or killed.

How They Bite

Sometime javelinas are thought to be rodents because of the nature of their teeth. Unlike rodents, which have 4 continually growing incisors, the sharp tusks of the javelina are actually their canine teeth. The tusks are self-sharpening. With each bite and chew the tusks rub against each other, creating a very sharp, chisel-like edge. Sometimes, when peccaries are threatened, they open their mouth and give a vocal warning by repeatedly clacking their upper and lower tusks together.

How Afraid Should I Be?

Javelinas almost always try to avoid contact with humans unless they are cornered or startled. When intimidated by a threat such as a dog or surprised by a human, the hair on their back will stand up, making them look larger and more threatening, and they may emit a strong, skunk-like smell from a specialized musk gland. If the javelina opens its mouth widely, displays its tusks and then repeatedly closes and opens its mouth eliciting a clacking sound, you should walk away. Sometimes in their haste to flee, confusion reigns and they haphazardly run toward people. This is not a charge but a frantic escape.

In some areas, javelinas have become habituated to humans, particularly if they learn that garbage cans hold delicious treats. These are smart animals and some people have actually trained individual javelinas to respond to a call or name. But one should remember, these are wild animals and if you push your luck in trying to make friends, you could be on the receiving end of a bite.

Preventing Javelina Bites

- Never approach or attempt to touch or feed a javelina. With their poor eyesight, they might accidentally flee right at you and accidentally cut you with their sharp tusks. And always keep some distance between you and the young reds (babies).

- If you encounter a herd while walking your dog, go the other way and keep your dog quiet. Javelinas always make a threat posture first. If that happens, leave the area. Don't encourage javelinas by leaving out food for them, or making dog food or water readily accessible. If one gets in an enclosed area, just open the gate and leave the area so it can find its way back out. Most bites result from deliberate feeding.

- Javelinas quickly learn that human garbage cans can provide some delicious treats and it doesn't take long for them to learn how to tip them

Thanks to Coyotes

- Coyote fur has been harvested for clothing for thousands of years.

- Coyotes feed heavily on many small rodents, squirrels and woodchucks, which are sometimes pests to agricultural crops.

- They are an important component of the rich biodiversity of the Southwest.

Myth Busters

MYTH: Coyotes that are out in the daytime are likely rabid.

Although coyotes active during the day could be rabid, it is not likely. More than likely such coyotes are healthy and simply feeding more than usual, particularly if there are young pups to feed.

MYTH: Coyotes kill mostly game animals.

This is a highly contentious issue in the Southwest. There are many who believe that coyotes have a negative impact on game, particularly deer populations. The controversy has put wildlife advocates at odds with those who want coyotes removed and highlights the divisiveness the coyote has brought to communities across the region. Research shows that coyotes in both urban and rural areas feed primarily on rodents. However, if given the opportunity, they will not turn down a white-tailed deer fawn or a clutch of pheasant eggs. And as Canada geese have flourished, some coyotes have learned to flush geese off their nests and steal the eggs.

Why They Bite

While hundreds of dog bites are reported each year in the Southwest, coyote bites are extremely rare. The natural instinct for a coyote that feels threatened is to flee or act defensively. Its best defensive weapons are its sharp teeth and its bite. While a coyote bite is very rare, a bite by a rabid coyote is even less common.

Animals that have become habituated to humans deliver almost all coyote bites. Often found around campgrounds and picnic areas, these coyotes should not be trusted.

How They Bite

Like other carnivorous mammals, coyotes have 4 sharp canine teeth and scissorlike shearing premolars called carnassials (the last upper premolars and the first lower molars).

These are adaptations for killing prey, and cutting and tearing meat, but they can also be used in self-defense. With their speed, relatively strong jaws and sharp teeth, coyotes are capable of delivering a nasty bite.

How Afraid Should I Be?

It is unlikely you or your family will be bitten by a coyote. A potentially dangerous coyote is one that becomes unafraid of humans. Normally these are shy, secretive animals. Most coyote bites happen in areas where they have become habituated to humans—particularly where humans are feeding them. Records of coyote attacks on humans show that when attacks do happen, children under the age of 5 are typically the likeliest to be attacked. You should be suspicious of any coyote that is acting boldly or aggressively.

RABIES

In the Southwest, the coyote is rarely a carrier of rabies. Bats, skunks and raccoons have a higher incidence of harboring rabies. For more information on rabies risks and precautions, see pp. 10–11.

Preventing Coyote Bites

- Never approach or attempt to touch a coyote.

- Reinforce a coyote's fear of humans by acting aggressively around them. Yell, throw sticks or stones and show your dominance by keeping direct eye contact.

- Discourage coyotes from hanging around your home. Uneaten food attracts unwanted visitors, including coyotes. Keep food garbage cleaned up. Make composted foods unavailable through proper screening, or place them in an enclosed composter.

- Keep small to midsize pets indoors, and if you feed larger pets outdoors, be sure that all uneaten food is cleaned up.

Treatment of Bites

- If you are bitten by a coyote, wash the wound, stop the bleeding with a compress, bandage it and seek medical attention. Since a coyote is a wild animal, you should contact the proper animal control agency and your doctor or the department of health for further advice.

- Puncture wounds should be thoroughly flushed and cleaned with a topical antibiotic. Deep puncture wounds require medical assistance.

- Watch for possible infection.

BOTTOM LINE

Most coyotes avoid humans, and attacks are extremely rare. The few bites reported have nearly always involved animals that have grown comfortable around humans and are unafraid of them. Coyotes hanging around campgrounds and picnic areas where ill-advised feeding occurs should not be trusted.

Gila Monsters

It's slow. It spends over 90 percent of its life underground. It would be really difficult to get this animal to bite you. However, with a surname of "monster" it's going to be difficult for people to love you even if your colorful skin and slow nature are more like a Mardi Gras float of sorts.

About Gila Monsters

With a surname of "monster" it's going to be difficult for people to love you. However, this colorful lizard is hardly a monster compared to the usual associations with the name—unless you happen to be a small prey species that finds itself in the solid grip of the mouth of this stout lizard. While it is the largest lizard in the United States, its shy nature makes sightings of this beautiful animal somewhat rare.

The Gila (pronounced hee-la) monster is a large docile lizard, and 1 of only a few venomous lizards in the entire world. The other is the larger Mexican beaded lizard, which is found primarily in Mexico and Guatemala.

Both male and female Gila monsters are covered in bands of colorful rounded, beadlike scales that range in color from black to pink and orange. Each scale covers a small bone particle. Consequently, the Gila monster's skin is a highly protective and tough covering. Unlike snakes and some lizards, the Gila monster does not shed its skin.

Their long curved claws enable them to crawl over rocks and even climb shrubs and small trees. Adult Gila monsters can measure up to 22 inches long and their thick tails allow them to store more energy reserves than other lizards.

Life and Times . . .

These colorful, desert-dwelling lizards are found in Arizona, near the southern edge of Nevada, in the southeastern corner of California and in the southwestern corners of Utah and New Mexico. They prefer arid, shrubby and rocky ground for habitat.

Rarely encountered, they prefer to spend most of their lives hidden underground. Hidden below the scorching desert surface, they can better conserve energy.

Gila monsters consume fairly large meals; sometimes up to one-third of their own body weight. Favorite foods include other smaller lizards, rodents, small birds, eggs and insects. Their slow metabolic rate, coupled with their ability to store fat reserves and their gluttonous eating habits allow them to lie low and rest often underground.

One is more likely to encounter a Gila monster over the 3 spring months from late April to early June. These normally solitary animals might be found with others during this period. Males, which tend to be slightly larger and more stocky than females, may battle for dominance in combative wrestling bouts. The winning males have the opportunity to mate with females.

After mating, females lay 2–12 leathery eggs that overwinter belowground and hatch 10 months later during the following spring. Hatchling lizards are about 6 inches long and are miniature, colorful replicas of their parents.

Fascinating Facts

- The first specimen of Gila monster collected by non-natives was an animal procured by Arthur Schott during a survey of the U.S.-Mexico border in 1855.

- The spring mating season also corresponds with bird nesting season and eggs from ground-nesting birds are a favorite food of this colorful lizard.

- While these sluggish and stubby lizards appear clumsy, their strong legs and long sharp claws enable them to climb trees and cacti in search of food.

Thanks to Gila Monsters

- Researchers are learning that Gila monsters are a rich component of a healthy biodiversity in the Southwest and significant medical knowledge could be lost if these amazing animals were to disappear. For example, a peptide component of Gila monster venom, called exendin-4, has been investigated for treating Type 2 diabetes. The peptide encourages the secretion of insulin during elevated blood glucose levels.

- American Indians of the Tohono O'odham and the Pima tribes believed that the lizard possessed a spiritual power capable of causing sickness. And the Seri and Yaquai tribes once believed in the healing powers of the Gila monster's hide.

Myth Busters

MYTH: If a Gila monster bites, it will not let go until sundown or until it thunders.

While this lizard has a firm and powerful grip when it bites, it has nothing to do with the weather or the time of the day.

MYTH: A Gila monster bite is always fatal.

Death from a Gila monster bite is almost unheard of. There is 1 alleged human fatality from the early 1930s, when a drunk man stuck his finger in a Gila monster's mouth.

THINK TWICE

Think twice before picking up this slow-moving lizard. While the Gila monster might appear slow, it is capable of delivering a quick bite.

Why They Bite

Since these reptiles feed primarily on rodents, eggs, nestling birds, and insects, biologists feel that their poison is used more for defense than for obtaining food. Gila monsters are hardly inconspicuous; they want to be seen. Similar to the bright coloration of a coral snake, the Gila monster's bright hues are a visual warning to "Look at me and stay back!"

These lizards will bite only when agitated. You have to really be careless to be on the receiving end of a Gila monster bite.

How They Bite

Unlike rattlesnakes, Gila monsters do not inject venom though hollow fangs. Instead, the delivery occurs via large grooved teeth in their lower jaw. The venom is stored in modified salivary glands. They cannot control the amount of venom released in each bite, but they can bite quickly and will stubbornly hold on and chew, rather than inject, the venom into the victim. The venom is moved through capillary action along the grooved teeth. Only a small amount of the poison is delivered during the bite.

How Afraid Should I Be?

Most people consider themselves lucky to see a Gila monster, given its reclusive nature and underground habitat. Due to their slow, sluggish nature and bright colors, it is easy to avoid them. You have to almost try to get bitten.

If encountered, stay back several feet from the animal. Your close presence will only stress out the lizard. Respect it from a distance.

While a bite from a Gila monster is incredibly unlikely, the venom is potent, similar to that of a western diamondback rattlesnake. While the bite from a Gila monster is not considered lethal, it can be quite painful. Consequently, these reptiles need to be highly respected.

Preventing Gila Monster Bites

- While Gila monsters are slow and sluggish, they can bite swiftly if necessary. For the most part they live underground, so they are rarely encountered. They are most likely observed during the mating season when they are searching for a mate. If you are lucky enough to see one, simply keep your distance.

- Handling a Gila monster is not suggested—but if you do so, handle it carefully and gently.

- Never harass or tease a Gila monster; you could provoke a bite.

- Do not reach into burrows or dens. A resting Gila monster or venomous snake could be residing there and be provoked to bite.

Treatment of Bites

- Remain calm.

- The best way to get the animal to loosen its strong biting grip is to calmly pry its mouth open. Use a pen, a pencil or a stick to do this. Avoid the urge to jerk or tear the lizard away. Calmly removing the biting lizard will result

Thanks to Cougars

- Besides being a prominent symbol of the wilderness, these amazing mammals are always a popular species of wildlife for humans to watch and photograph.

- They are an important component to the rich biodiversity of the Southwest and a key player in predator-prey relationships.

Myth Busters

MYTH: Cougars will attack people if the conditions are right (or wrong).

Less than 1 percent of cougars will "lock on" to humans as potential prey. And these animals usually have some physical problem or illness that makes them inefficient hunters.

MYTH: Cougars will leap from trees on their prey.

While cougars are extremely stealthy, they depend primarily on their ability to stalk and pursue with a burst of speed—all from the ground.

Why They Bite

Cougars will usually go out of their way to avoid humans. But there are instances when cougars have preyed on humans. Most reported attacks on humans are predatory; they are seeking food.

How They Bite and Claw

Cougars usually move rapidly toward their prey with a burst of speed before leaping on the prey's back. They then bite down on the neck of their prey and sever the spine. On larger animals they sometimes reach around the snout of the animal, pulling its head back and breaking its neck.

Like other carnivorous mammals, cougars have 4 sharp canine teeth and scissorlike shearing premolars called carnassials (the last upper premolars and first lower molars). These are adaptations for killing prey and cutting and tearing food, but they work well as defensive weapons. With their quickness, exceptionally strong jaws and sharp teeth, cougars are capable of inflicting a serious bite.

Like other cats, cougars also have very sharp claws. Unlike canines, which have fixed claws, a cougar's claws are retractable. In other words, the claws are hidden until the cat's paw is stretched out. When the paw relaxes, the tendon in the foot relaxes and the claws are pulled in. The sharp claws allow the cougar to easily climb trees and they are useful in attacking prey.

How Afraid Should I Be?

While it is true that cougars sometimes kill livestock, pets and even humans, it's unlikely that you'll see one in the wild, let alone be attacked. Over the past 120 years there have been 21 documented human deaths as a result of cougar attacks, with 11 since 1990. Biologists feel that this increase is due to a couple factors. First, the overall human population has increased, and there has been a subsequent increase in the amount of people spending time hiking, mountain biking, backpacking, fishing, hunting and running in cougar habitat. Second, in many areas of cougar habitat there has been an increase in prey animals, particularly deer, leading to a rise in the cougar population.

THINK TWICE

Think twice if you see a cougar that is unafraid of humans. A normal cougar should be very afraid of a human. If you see such unusual behavior, contact the U.S. Fish and Wildlife Service.

To put your chances of being attacked by a cougar in perspective, consider this: approximately 115 people die every day in vehicle crashes in the United States. That is roughly 1 death every 13 minutes. And yet we don't cower in fear each time we get into a car, but many people are instinctively (and perhaps irrationally) afraid of cougars and other wild animals.

Preventing Cougar Bites and Scratches

- Never approach or attempt to touch a cougar.

- Discourage cougars from hanging around your home or cabin by keeping pets indoors, keeping pet food indoors and being sure that all uneaten pet food is cleaned up.

- Keep children close to you when in cougar habitat. If a cougar is sighted, be sure to place yourself between the cougar and the child. *Never* tell the child to run to you. The cougar might be triggered to pursue the fleeing "prey."

- If you see a cougar, don't run or turn your back. It's hardwired to chase fleeing animals.

- Stand up tall, and if necessary, raise your arms high. You want to look as big and imposing as possible. Be aggressive. Yell, shout, throw rocks or sticks toward the cougar. If attacked, do not relax and play dead. Be aggressive and fight with whatever is at hand—a club, a stick, a rock, a hiking stick, or even your bare hands.

- At night, use a bright flashlight to scare a cougar away.

- Move slowly away from the cougar and leave the area or seek shelter.

Treatment of Bites

- If you are bitten or clawed by a cougar, contact a doctor immediately and the local department of health. Also be sure to contact the U.S. Fish and Wildlife Service to inform them a cougar attack has occurred in the area.

- If it's not a serious wound, treat it as you would a dog or cat bite. Puncture wounds or scratch injuries should be flushed and thoroughly cleansed with a topical antibiotic. Deep punctures, gashes and other serious wounds require medical assistance.

- Watch for possible infection of the bite.

BOTTOM LINE

Cougars usually go out of their way to avoid humans. It's unlikely that you'll even see a cougar in the Southwest. Consider yourself very lucky if you see one.

Black Bears

Among indigenous cultures, few wild animals have held such a place of honor as the black bear. They were held sacred and to be offered "bear medicine" was a highly revered gift. Perhaps we need to keep in mind the American Indian concept of Bear Medicine—to practice introspection and take in all the facts, give it critical thought and then act.

I had not originally intended to include the black bear in this book. However, when I surveyed outdoor professionals and enthusiasts about which creatures to cover, the black bear kept popping up as an animal that strikes fear into the hearts of many folks. You know the familiar mantra, "Lions and tigers and bears. Oh my!" We have grown up with this fear constantly being taught to us.

About Black Bears

Historically, black bears and grizzly bears were found in part of the Southwest, but now only black bears are found here. Black bears are native to the higher elevations and forested areas of the Southwest. In Nevada they are found primarily in the national, state and tribal forests on the western edge of the state.

True to their name, black bears are usually black, though occasionally they are brown, tan or cinnamon. Bears are omnivores, and these opportunistic feeders feed on a wide variety of foods, including plant foliage, berries, fruit, roots, fish, insects, small mammals and sometimes young ungulates (hoofed animals such as deer, elk and antelope). According to bear studies in British Columbia, plants make up 90 percent of their diet. When presented with the opportunity, they also feed on human garbage, birdseed and, yes, even camp food.

As the black bear population grows, more people are seeing these magnificent beasts. Yet the greatest threat to bears is loss of habitat. As humans continue to build homes and cabins in bear country, the likelihood of encounters with bears is greater. Unfortunately, any bear that shows up looking for food is considered a nuisance or a threat and such bears are often shot.

Life and Times . . .

In the Southwest, these specialized hibernators usually den up for winter in late November and early December. Unlike some mammal hibernators such as the woodchuck or ground squirrel, a bear's winter body temperature does not change dramatically from its summer body temperature. During the winter months, a female bear gives birth to 2 or 3 cubs. Each cub weighs less than a pound at birth. She is able to nurse the bears on high-fat milk that she produces from her stores of body fat. The cubs generally stay with their mother for 2 winters before going off on their own.

By the end of March and early April, the bears are on the move and begin looking for food. Their mating season takes place in early summer around the month of June. The bear's primary job in summer and early fall is to eat; during these seasons they must consume 1 year's worth of food in 6 months.

Fascinating Facts

- The black bear is the most widespread of the 3 North American bear species. The other 2 species are the grizzly bear (also called the brown bear) and the polar bear.

- While an adult human might consume an average of 1,500 calories per day, the black bear can consume 30,000 calories per day when readying itself for hibernation! Imagine eating 20 times more than an average adult human male!

- Bears and dogs are close relatives. Taxonomists believe that they shared a common ancestor.

- A bear's normal heartbeat on a summer day is 50–90 beats per minute. During hibernation, it only beats about 8 times a minute!

- Bears have an amazing sense of smell and can hone in on faint smells from a long distance. In fact, 100 percent of reported home invasions by bears in Nevada have been into the kitchen area.

Thanks to Black Bears

- Besides being a prominent symbol of wild regions, many people enjoy seeing black bears in the wild.

- As omnivores, bears are members of the cleanup crew in the wilderness. They will not pass up the opportunity to scavenge on dead animals.

- Bears are an important component of the biodiversity of the Southwest.

Myth Busters

MYTH: If you encounter a black bear, particularly a mother and cubs, you will be attacked.

There is a common legend that black bears, especially black bear mothers, attack any humans they see. That's simply not true. Black bears very rarely attack. It's highly unlikely that they will attack you, even if you are near a mother and her cubs. But that doesn't mean

you should take the chance. If you see any black bears, keep to a safe distance. They may be shy, but they are still powerful creatures.

MYTH: When a black bear stomps its feet and bluffs a charge, it is preparing to attack.

Their most common aggressive displays are merely rituals that they perform when they are nervous; this includes fake charges. It's far more likely that bears will run away or seek safety in a tree.

Why They Bite

It's highly unlikely that you'll be bitten by a black bear. If bears have any impact on you at all, it's far more likely that bears will damage your campsite, camping gear, bird feeding station, garden or beehives. A friend who lived in grizzly and black bear country always liked to see a summer of good wild berry production. He would always say, "Good berries mean the bears are happy." Bears are essentially eating machines, and they need to put on amazing fat reserves for the upcoming winter. The expression, "I'm as hungry as a bear," is especially accurate when one considers how much fat bears put on for the upcoming winter. Some bears are capable of adding 90 pounds of fat per month for 3 months in preparation for winter. After gaining nearly 100 pounds, an adult male bear will lose up to 30 percent of its body weight while hibernating.

When natural foods such as berries are scarce, bears become bolder and are attracted to our foods and gardens. Unfortunately, this often results in more human/bear conflicts and consequently it means more bruins are killed as "nuisance bears."

How They Bite

Black bears have powerful jaws with a full set of teeth, and they also have sharp claws, particularly on their front feet. These tools not only help them eat a wide range of foods, but they can serve as weaponry if needed. It should be noted, however, that most bear-related injuries are not major life-threatening episodes.

How Afraid Should I Be?

It's very unlikely that you'll be on the receiving end of a bear bite. You are far more likely to get killed riding your bicycle or drowning while swimming—and these are considered healthy pastimes.

Interestingly, an average of 1 person is killed in the United States each year by bears of all species. In contrast, white-tailed deer are responsible for more than 150 human deaths each year (deer/car collisions), and dogs kill an average of 15–20 people a year in our country. The reality is that the media seems to thrive on large animal attacks—while joggers and cyclists who encounter "attacks" from motorists rarely get the same onslaught of news coverage.

Preventing Black Bear Bites

- Remember, food is the primary reason that bears and humans encounter each other. Keep a clean campsite to minimize bear conflicts. Do not keep food scraps or garbage sitting out and don't dump them near your campsite. Don't clean fish or game near your camp.

- Whether you are car camping or primitive camping, keep all your food sealed in airtight containers or plastic bags to minimize bear encounters. And do all your food prep and cooking well away from your tents.

- The best protection in bear country is awareness of bears and their behavior. Watch for signs of bears in order to avoid encounters, and be sure to understand the defensive behaviors of bears (such as a bluff charge). This will help avoid an ugly bear encounter.

- When hiking in bear country it is best to hike in groups of 4 or more. And be talkative or sing songs. The idea is to never surprise a bear.

THINK TWICE

Think twice about setting up your picnic or camp near garbage cans or other human refuse.

Think twice before trying to get a photo of a "cute" campground bear. Black bears that are used to people cannot be trusted.

- Never camp in areas where there is evidence of bears feeding nearby. Such clues might include torn-up logs or ant mounds, the smell of carrion or signs of bear diggings. Also, avoid camping in areas where you find bear droppings; particularly those that contain bits and pieces of plastic or paper packaging.

- If a bear approaches your camp, it is best if you and any others with you can appear as a mob of humans and make noise. This means yelling and banging pots and pans. But keep your distance and allow the bear an avenue of escape.

- Sometimes black bears will bluff charge. In such cases, the bear starts to charge, but then stops suddenly. If this happens, stand your ground, then back away slowly, talking calmly.

- In some areas in bear country, campsites have metal bear-proof lockers for food storage. Properly hanging your food out of reach of bears can also protect it (and you). The U.S. Forest Service recommends that you hang food at least 12 feet off the ground and 10 feet away from the nearest tree trunk.

IF ATTACKED . . .

- If you have a firearm, use it as a last resort. If you have pepper spray, be sure to use it according to directions and remember that the spray is most effective at 10–15 feet, so don't spray it too early.

- *Never* run away or scream. Your fleeing might only trigger a more aggressive attack.

- If a black bear attacks you, it is best to aggressively fight back.

PEPPER SPRAY USE AGAINST AGGRESSIVE BEARS

Ideally, if you are well versed about bears, you will never have to use pepper spray. The main ingredient in the cloud of dispersed bear spray is a derivative of capsicum, an oil derived from red peppers. It affects the upper respiratory system and triggers an intense burning sensation in the eyes. Always buy spray that is labeled "bear deterrent spray."

Treatment of Bites

If you or someone in your party receives a bear bite or is scratched by a bear's claws, first determine the severity of the injury.

- Clean all non-life-threatening injuries and seek medical attention. Even if the wound is superficial, it is wise to seek medical assistance to help properly clean the wound.

- If there is abundant bleeding, apply pressure to the wound and call 911 for medical assistance.

BOTTOM LINE

It is highly unlikely that a black bear will attack you. Humans attack and kill their fellow humans at a rate more than 90,000 times that of bears harming us. Enjoy seeing these amazing animals, but stay a safe, nonthreatening distance away. Food is the primary reason bears cause problems for humans (such as tipped-over garbage cans or ransacked camps). Keeping a clean yard and campsite will greatly reduce the likelihood of bear problems.

Glossary

anaphylactic shock an extreme, often life-threatening, allergic reaction to an antigen (e.g., a bee sting) to which the body has become hypersensitive following an earlier exposure (pp. 10, 34–35)

anticoagulant a substance with the ability to slow or inhibit the clotting of blood (pp. 39, 51, 88)

bacterium a member of a large group of single-celled microorganisms that have cell walls but lack specialized structures and a nucleus; some, not all, can cause disease (pp. 25–27, 52)

carnassials the large upper premolar and lower molar teeth of a carnivore, adapted for shearing/cutting flesh (pp. 108, 121, 134, 145)

carnivore an animal that eats other animals (pp. 70, 108, 121, 134, 144–145)

cephalothorax the fused head and thorax of spiders (pp. 43, 46)

chelicerae a pair of appendages that look like legs that are found in front of the mouth of spiders and other arachnids; they are usually pincerlike claws (pg. 45)

compound eye an eye consisting of many small visual units, typically found in insects and crustaceans such as certain shrimp (pg. 50)

DEET an abbreviation for an insect repellent called diethyl-meta-toluamide, a colorless, oily liquid with a mild odor, the chemical effectively "blinds" the insect's senses, so the biting/feeding instinct is not triggered (pp. 15, 27, 40)

delayed fertilization a significant delay (longer than the minimum time required for sperm to travel to the egg) between copulation and fertilization; used to describe female sperm storage (pg. 79)

eastern equine encephalitis a viral disease carried by mosquitoes (pg. 39)

echolocation the location of objects by reflected sound (echo), particularly used by dolphins, whales and bats (pp. 84–85, 87)

ecdysis when an organism, such as a rattlesnake, sheds its skin (pg. 87)

EpiPen a combined syringe and needle that injects a single dose of medication to counteract anaphylactic shock (pp. 10, 61, 67)

estrus a period of fertility when many female mammals are receptive to sexual intercourse (pp. 126, 131, 143–144)

exoskeleton a hardened or rigid external body covering found on some invertebrate animals; it provides both support and protection (pp. 34, 73)

hibernation a physical condition of dormancy and inactivity that is an effective strategy for conserving energy during weather extremes such as winter; the metabolism is greatly reduced, often resulting in a lower body temperature, slower breathing and reduced heart rate (pp. 79–80, 90, 115, 120, 149–151)

Jacobson's organ a scent organ commonly found on the roof of the mouth of snakes and lizards (pg. 102)

lancet a small double-edged knife or blade with a sharp point (pg. 59)

Lyme disease a bacterial infection caused by the bite of an infected tick (pp. 23, 25–26, 28–29)

larva the immature form of an insect (pp. 13–14, 17–19, 23, 31–33, 37–38, 50–51, 55–57, 63, 69, 123)

neurotoxin a poison or toxin that affects the nervous system (pp. 26, 46, 96)

omnivore an animal that eats both plants and animals (pp. 33, 107, 113, 119, 149–150)

ovipositor the slender, tubular organ through which a female insect deposits eggs (pp. 57–58)

ovulate the release of ova (egg cells) from the ovary (pg. 79)

parasite an organism that gains nourishment from others (pp. 18, 123)

pedipalps specialized appendages, resembling legs, that are attached to an arachnid's cephalothorax; in scorpions, they are pincers; in spiders, they are sensory organs (pp. 43, 74–75)

permethrin a synthetic insecticide of the pyrethroid class, used primarily against disease-carrying insects (pp. 27, 40)

pheromone a chemical substance that triggers a natural behavioral response in another member of the same species (pp. 32, 43, 66, 74)

pupa an insect in its inactive immature form, between larva and adult, such as in the chrysalis stage (pp. 13–14, 37, 50, 56, 63)

rabies a viral disease that invades the central nervous system of mammals, including humans (pp. 10–11, 81–83, 109, 111, 121–123, 129, 134)

spermatophore a protein capsule containing a mass of spermatozoa, which is transferred during mating in various insects, arthropods and some mollusks (pg. 74)

spirochete a flexible, spiral-shaped bacterium (pg. 26)

stylostome the channel-like structure that is formed by chiggers when feeding on a host's surface (pp. 18–19)

thorax the middle section of the body of an insect, between the head and the abdomen, bearing the legs and wings (pp. 31, 70)

viable a seed, egg or embryo that is capable of growing and developing (pp. 32, 51)

viviparous bringing forth live young that have developed inside the body of the parent (pp. 74, 87)

West Nile virus a viral disease contracted through the bite of a mosquito; the disease interferes with the central nervous system and causes inflammation of brain tissue (pp. 39, 41)

References

NO-SEE-UMS

"Biting Flies." Koehler, Philip G. and F. M. Oi. Institute of Food and Agricultural Sciences Extension, #ENY-220, April 1991. University of Florida, Electronic Data Information Source: http://edis.ifas.ufl.edu/ig081

"Biting Midges." Rutledge-Connelly, C. Roxanne. Featured Creatures, EENY-349, May 2005. University of Florida: http://entnemdept.ufl.edu/creatures/aquatic/biting_midges.htm

"Bluetongue Virus." McDill, Lisa. Indiana Animal Disease Diagnostic Laboratory, Spring 2002 Newsletter. Purdue University: http://www.addl.purdue.edu/newsletters/2002/spring/bluetongue.shtml

"Ceratopogonidae." Wikipedia, The Free Encyclopedia: http://en.wikipedia.org/wiki/Ceratopogonidae

McCafferty, W. Frank. *Aquatic Entomology: The Fishermen's Guide and Ecologists' Illustrated Guide to Insects and Their Relatives.* Jones and Bartlett Publishers, 1991.

"Sand Fly - No Seeum Control." U-Spray, Inc.: http://www.bugspray.com/article/sandflies.html

CHIGGERS

"Biology and Control of Chiggers." Cilek, James E. and Eric T. Schreiber. Public Health Entomology Research and Education Center, *EntGuide*, EG#6. Florida A&M University: http://pherec.org/EntGuides/EntGuide6.pdf

"Chigger." Study of Northern Virginia Ecology, Island Creek Elementary School. Fairfax County Public Schools: http://www.fcps.edu/islandcreekes/ecology/chigger.htm

"Chiggers." Koehler, Philip G. and F. M. Oi. Institute of Food and Agricultural Sciences Extension, #ENY-212, May 1991. University of Florida, Electronic Data Information Source: http://edis.ifas.ufl.edu/IG085

"Chiggers." Moore, Glen C. and M. E. Merchant. AgriLife Extension, E-365, November 2005. Texas A&M University: http://insects.tamu.edu/extension/publications/epubs/e-365.cfm

"Chiggers: Description of Chiggers, Elimination of Chiggers." Professional Pest Control Products: http://www.pestproducts.com/chiggers.htm

"Chiggers in Florida." Wild Florida Ecotravel Guide: http://www.wildflorida.com/articles/Chiggers_in_Florida.php

"Mystery Bites and Itches - Arthropod and Non-Arthropod Sources in Colorado." Cranshaw, Whitney S. Colorado State University Extension: http://www.ext.colostate.edu/pubs/insect/bug_bites.html

TICKS

"About Human Anaplasmosis." Minnesota Department of Health: http://www.health.state.mn.us/divs/idepc/diseases/anaplasmosis/basics.html

"Advanced Topics in Lyme Disease: Diagnostic Hints and Treatment Guidelines for Lyme and other Tick Borne Illnesses." Burrascano, Joseph J. Jr., M.D. "Managing Lyme Disease, Fifteenth Edition," September 2005. International Lyme and Associated Diseases Society: http://www.ilads.org/files/burrascano_0905.pdf

Article about Lyme disease in Montana from the *Missoulian*, March 2004. Merriam, Ginny. Canadian Lyme Disease Foundation. CanLyme: http://www.canlyme.com/montanalyme.html

"Blacklegged Tick or Deer Tick." Patnaude, Michael R. Featured Creatures, EENY-143, July 2000. University of Florida: http://entnemdept.ufl.edu/creatures/urban/medical/deer_tick.htm

"Colorado Tick Fever." Bureau of Epidemiology, August 2001. Utah Department of Health: http://health.utah.gov/epi/fact_sheets/ctf.html

"Colorado Tick Fever." MedlinePlus: http://www.nlm.nih.gov/medlineplus/ency/article/000675.htm

"Deer Ticks and Lyme Disease on Cape Cod and the Islands." Brochure provided by Barnstable County Department of Health and the Environment, Barnstable, MA.

Drummond, Roger. *Ticks And What You Can Do About Them.* Wilderness Press, 1990.

"Evaluation of a Tick Bite for Possible Lyme Disease." Sexton, Daniel J. UpToDate, Inc.: http://www. uptodate.com/contents/evaluation-of-a-tick-bite-for-possible-lyme-disease?

Guilfoile, Patrick. *Ticks Off! Controlling Ticks That Transmit Lyme Disease on Your Property.* ForSte Press, Inc., 2004.

"How Can I Avoid Ticks Carrying Lyme Disease? Lake Home & Cabin Kit, Second Edition." University of Minnesota Extension Service Faculty, 2006. University of Minnesota Extension: http://4h.umn.edu/ distribution/naturalresources/components/DD8241_8.pdf

"Idaho Tick Types." Lahl, Jennifer. eHow: http://www.ehow.com/list_6893024_idaho-tick-types.html

"Known Vectors That Transmit Lyme Disease are Ticks." Canadian Lyme Disease Foundation. CanLyme: http://www.canlyme.com/ticks.html

Knutson, Roger M. *Furtive Fauna: A Field Guide to the Creatures Who Live On You.* Penguin Books, 1992.

"Lots Of Links On Lyme Disease." Reocities: http://www.reocities.com/HotSprings/Oasis/6455/

"Lyme Disease." Shiel, William C. Jr., M.D., F.A.C.P., F.A.C.R. MedicineNet, Inc. WebMD: http://www. medicinenet.com/lyme_disease/article.htm

"Lyme Disease in Interior Western States." November 2010. The Kaiser Papers: http://lyme.kaiserpapers. org/lyme-disease-in-interior-western-states.html

"MedlinePlus." U.S. National Library of Medicine. National Institutes of Health: http://www.nlm.nih.gov/ medlineplus/medlineplus.html

"Mosquito and Tick-Borne Diseases: Rocky Mountain Spotted Fever." Perlin, David, Ph.D. and Ann Cohen. *The Complete Idiot's Guide to Dangerous Diseases and Epidemics*, 2002. Infoplease: http://www.infoplease.com/ cig/dangerous-diseases-epidemics/rocky-mountain-spotted-fever.html

"Rocky Mountain Spotted Fever." Colorado Department of Public Health and Environment, Disease Control and Environmental Epidemiology Division. Colorado, The Official State Web Portal: http://www.cdphe.state. co.us/dc/zoonosis/tick/rmsfinfo.html

"Rocky Mountain Wood Tick." Green Valley Pest Control: http://www.greenvalleypc.com/html/ticks/rocky.htm

"Signs and Symptoms of Lyme Disease." Centers for Disease Control and Prevention: http://www.cdc.gov/ lyme/signs_symptoms/index.html

"Tickborne Disease & Daylight Savings Time Arrive Together in Montana." Montana Public Health, Vol. 2, Added Issue, April 2007. Internet Archive: http://ia600508.us.archive.org/4/items/2D9FD079-6FE7-40D0-AE35-F4251F74E076/2D9FD079-6FE7-40D0-AE35-F4251F74E076.pdf

"Tick-Borne Diseases in Montana." Montana Integrated Pest Management Center, Yard and Garden Weeds, Insects, Diseases, December 2001. Montana State University Extension: http://ipm.montana.edu/ YardGarden/docs/ticks-insect.htm

"Tickborne Diseases of the U.S." Centers for Disease Control and Prevention: http://www.cdc.gov/ticks/ diseases/

"Tick-Borne Diseases: Relapsing Fever." Colorado Department of Public Health and Environment, Disease Control and Environmental Epidemiology Division. Colorado, The Official State Web Portal: http://www. cdphe.state.co.us/dc/zoonosis/tick/relapinfo.html

"Tick Borne Relapsing Fever." Centers for Disease Control and Prevention: http://www.cdc.gov/ncidod/ dvbid/RelapsingFever/index.htm

"Ticks." Foley, Ian A. Montana Fish, Wildlife & Parks. Montana's Official State Website: http://fwp.mt.gov/ recreation/safety/wildlife/ticks/

"Ticks and Tick-borne Diseases." New Mexico Department of Health: http://www.health.state.nm.us/erd/HealthData/documents/Ticks_001.pdf

"Ticks in Colorado." Julian, Joe. Colorado Master Gardener, 2010. Colorado State University Extension: http://www.colostate.edu/Dept/CoopExt/4dmg/Pests/ticks.htm

"Tularemia." Health Beat. Illinois Department of Public Health: http://www.idph.state.il.us/public/hb/hbtulare.htm

"Utah Lyme Disease Support Group." About Lyme Disease. UtahLyme: http://www.utahlyme.org./

"With Warmer Days Coming, Residents Reminded to Avoid Ticks." News from Wyoming Department of Health, April 2010. Wyoming Department of Health: http://m.health.wyo.gov/news.aspx?NewsID=380

"Wyoming Department of Health Warns About Tick-Borne Diseases." May 2007. HighBeam Research: http://www.highbeam.com/doc/1P3-1269096921.html

FIRE ANTS

"Fire Ant." Wikipedia, The Free Encyclopedia: http://en.wikipedia.org/wiki/Fire_ant

"Fire Ant Bite Home Remedies." FireAnt: http://www.fireant.net/Bites/index.php

"Fire Ants, Armadillos, and Phorid Flies - Answers to Frequently Asked Questions." Gilbert, Larry E. December 2004. The University of Texas at Austin: http://uts.cc.utexas.edu/~gilbert/research/fireants/faqans.html

"How Can I Avoid Being Stung by Fire Ants?" Gilbert, Larry E. "Fire Ants, Armadillos, and Phorid Flies - Answers to Frequently Asked Questions," December 2004. http://uts.cc.utexas.edu/~gilbert/research/fireants/faqans.html#avoid

"Killing Ants, Fireants with Grits." Professional Pest Control Products: http://www.pestproducts.com/grits.htm

Taber, Stephen Welton. *Fire Ants*. Texas A&M University Press, 2000.

MOSQUITOES

"Disease Maps." Eastern Equine Encephalitis Human 2011: Montana. U.S. Geological Survey: http://diseasemaps.usgs.gov/eee_mt_human.html

"Disease Maps." West Nile Virus Human 2011: Idaho. U.S. Geological Survey: http://diseasemaps.usgs.gov/wnv_id_human.html

"Mosquito Management (Supplement to Fact Sheet 5.526)." Peairs, Frank B. and Whitney S. Cranshaw. Colorado State University Extension: http://www.ext.colostate.edu/westnile/mosquito_mgt.html

Spielman, Andrew, Sc.D. and Michael D'Antonio. *Mosquito: A Natural History of Our Most Persistent and Deadly Foe*. Hyperion, 2001.

"Tips For Treating Mosquito Bites." Green, Alan, M.D. F.A.A.P. July 1998. Dr. Greene: http://www.drgreene.com

"West Nile Virus and Mosquito-Borne Viruses in Colorado: Frequently Asked Questions." Colorado Department of Public Health and Environment, Disease Control and Environmental Epidemiology Division. Colorado, The Official State Web Portal: http://www.cdphe.state.co.us/dc/zoonosis/wnv/westnilefaq.html

"What is West Nile Virus?" Preventive Health and Safety Division. Wyoming Department of Health: http://www.health.wyo.gov/phsd/skeeter/whatisWNV.html

"What's Eating You? — July - August 2001." Weber, Larry. *Minnesota Conservation Volunteer*, July–August 2001. Minnesota Department of Natural Resources: http://www.dnr.state.mn.us/young_naturalists/biting_bugs/index.html

Wolff, Theodore A. and Lewis T. Nielsen. *The Mosquitoes of New Mexico*. University of New Mexico Press, 2007.

SPIDERS

"Brown Recluse Spiders in Colorado: Recognition and Spiders of Similar Appearance." Cranshaw, Whitney S. Fact Sheet No. 5.607, February 2008. Colorado State University Extension: http://www.ext.colostate.edu/pubs/insect/05607.html

Correspondence with Dr. David B. Richman, College Professor and Curator of The Arthropod Museum at New Mexico State University, Email: rdavid@nmsu.edu

Correspondence with Dr. Paula E. Cushing, Director of the American Arachnological Society, Denver Museum of Nature & Science, 2001 Colorado Boulevard, Denver, CO 80205-5798, Phone: 303.370.6442

"How to Identify Spiders in Colorado." Boston, David. eHow: http://www.ehow.com/how_4547848_identify-spiders-colorado.html

"Montana Spiders and Arachnids." Montana State University Extension: http://diagnostics.montana.edu/spider/

"Mystery Bites and Itches - Arthropod and Non-Arthropod Sources in Colorado." Cranshaw, Whitney S. Colorado State University Extension: http://www.ext.colostate.edu/pubs/insect/bug_bites.html

"Myth: Idiopathic Wounds are Often Due to Brown Recluse or Other Spider Bites Throughout the United States." Vetter, Richard S. PubMed Central, *The Western Journal of Medicine*, Vol. 173, November 2000. National Center for Biotechnology Information: http://www.ncbi.nlm.nih.gov/pmc/articles/PMC1071166/

"Spiders." Akre, Roger D., Ph.D., E. Paul Catts, Ph.D. and A. L. Antonelli, Ph.D. Insect Answers, EB1548, November 1997. Washington State University Extension: http://cru.cahe.wsu.edu/CEPublications/eb1548/eb1548.html

"USA Spider Identification Chart." Termite: http://www.termite.com/spider-identification.html

"Venomous Spiders Found in Each State." George, David W. Venombyte: http://www.venombyte.com/venom/spiders/venomous_spiders_by_state.asp

DEER AND HORSE FLIES

"Bites and Stings." Professional Pest Control Products: www.pestproducts.com/bitesandstings.htm

"Biting Flies." Koehler, Philip G. and F. M. Oi. Institute of Food and Agricultural Sciences Extension, #ENY-220, April 1991. University of Florida, Electronic Data Information Source: http://edis.ifas.ufl.edu/ig081

"Horse and Deer Flies: Biology and Public Health Risk." Hill, Catherine A. and John F. MacDonald. Public Health, Department of Entomology, E-246-W. Purdue Extension, Purdue University: http://extension.entm.purdue.edu/publications/E-246.pdf

Klots, Elsie B. *The New Field Book of Freshwater Life*. Putnam Publishing Group, 1966.

"Learn to Live With and Respect Horse Flies and Deer Flies." Murphree, Steve. *The Tennessee Conservationist*, Vol. LXXII, No. 4, July/August 2006. The Tennessee Conservationist, Tennessee Government: http://www.tn.gov/environment/tn_consv/archive/flies.pdf

McCafferty, W. Frank. *Aquatic Entomology: The Fishermen's Guide and Ecologists' Illustrated Guide to Insects and Their Relatives*. Jones and Bartlett Publishers, 1991

HORNETS, WASPS, YELLOW JACKETS AND HONEYBEES

"Ants, Bees, and Wasps." Household and Pantry Pests, Fact Sheets. Virginia Tech: http://www.insectid.ento.vt.edu/fact-sheets/household-pantry-pests/index.html

"Controlling Bald-faced Hornets and Yellowjackets in and Around Structures." Bambara, Stephen B. and Michael Waldvogel. Residential, Structural and Community Pests, Insect Note - ENT/rsc-10. North Carolina State University: http://www.ces.ncsu.edu/depts/ent/notes/Urban/horn-yj.htm

Everett Clinic, The: http://www.everettclinic.com/health-library.ashx?1300/topic/symptom/insbt/overview.htm

"Foraging Yellowjackets." Potter, Michael F. College of Agriculture, Department of Entomology, Entfact-634. The University of Kentucky: http://www.ca.uky.edu/entomology/entfacts/ef634.asp

"How to Get Rid of Yellow Jackets / Yellow Jacket Control." Do-It-Yourself Pest Control: http://doyourownpestcontrol.com/yellowjackets.htm

"Paper Wasps and Hornets." Lyon, William F. and Wegner, Gerald S. Ohio State University Extension Fact Sheet, Entomology, HYG-2077-97. The Ohio State University: http://ohioline.osu.edu/hyg-fact/2000/2077.html

"Pollination." eBeeHoney: http://www.ebeehoney.com/Pollination.html

Scott, Susan and Craig Thomas, M.D. *Pests of Paradise: First Aid and Medical Treatment of Injuries from Hawaii's Animals.* University of Hawaii Press, 2000.

Stokes, Donald W. *A Guide to Observing Insect Lives: Stokes Nature Guides.* Little, Brown and Company, 1983.

GIANT DESERT CENTIPEDES

"Animal Fact Sheet: Desert Centipede." Especially for Kids, 2008. Arizona-Sonora Desert Museum: http://www.desertmuseum.org/kids/oz/long-fact-sheets/Desert%20Centipede.php

"Centipede Bite Causes Pain, Inflammation." Thygerson, Alton. June 1995. Deseret News: http://www.deseretnews.com/article/422044/CENTIPEDE-BITE-CAUSES-PAIN-INFLAMMATION.html

"Centipede Envenomation." Norris, Robert L., M.D. Reference: Drugs, Diseases & Procedures. Medscape: http://emedicine.medscape.com/article/769448-overview

"Centipede, Millipede." AgriLife Extension, A Field Guide to Common Texas Insects, E-379. Texas A&M University: http://insects.tamu.edu/fieldguide/cimg379.html

"Centipedes." Hodgson, Erin W., Paul Bingham and Alan H. Roe. Utah Pests Fact Sheet, ENT-53-08, June 2008. Utah State University Extension: http://extension.usu.edu/files/publications/factsheet/ENT-53-08.pdf

"Centipedes & Millipedes." Lizotte, Renée. Arizona-Sonora Desert Museum: http://www.desertmuseum.org/books/nhsd_centipede.php

First Class Pest Control: http://www.firstclasspest.com/

Hare, Trevor. *Poisonous Dwellers of the Desert: Description, Habitat, Prevention, Treatment.* Southwest Parks and Monuments Association, 1995.

"Scolopendridae: Giant Centipede (*Scolopendra heros*); Newport, 1844." Giant Desert Centipede, April 2010. Bugs In The News: http://bugsinthenews.info/?p=1145

SCORPIONS

"Correspondence on 11/18/10 with Dr. David B. Richman, College Professor and Curator of the Arthropod Museum at New Mexico State University, Email: rdavid@nmsu.edu

"Scorpions of The USA: Checklists by State." McWest, Kari J. Kari's Scorpion Pages: http://www.angelfire.com/tx4/scorpiones/states.html

BATS

Adams, Rick A. *Bats of the Rocky Mountain West: Natural History, Ecology, and Conservation.* University Press of Colorado, 2004.

"Bats of Colorado." Colorado Bat Working Group. Colorado State University: http://www.cnhp.colostate.edu/teams/zoology/cbwg/batList.asp

"Bats of Utah, The: A Literature Review." Oliver, George V. State of Utah, Department of Natural Resources, Division of Wildlife Resources—Utah Natural Heritage Program, Publication No. 00–14, April 2000. Utah DNR: http://www.dwrcdc.nr.utah.gov/ucdc/viewreports/bats.pdf

Wilson, Don E. *Bats in Question: The Smithsonian Answer Book.* Smithsonian Institution Press, 1997.

SNAKES

"Checklist of Idaho Reptiles." Peterson, Charles R. June 1997. Idaho State University: http://www.isu. edu/~petechar/idar/idahoreptileschecklist.html

"Checklist of Montana Amphibians and Reptiles Amphibians." Faculty Web Pages. Montana State University Billings: http://www.msubillings.edu/ScienceFaculty/handouts/Spring%202006/Barron/Biol%20460/ Checklist%20of%20Montana%20Amphibians%20and%20Reptiles.pdf

Colorado Herpetological Society: http://www.coloherps.org/

"Colorado's Snakes." Colorado Herpetological Society: http://www.coloherps.org/reference/sort_snakes.htm

"Coping With Snakes." Cerato, M. and W. F. Andelt. Fact Sheet No. 6.501, May 2006. Colorado State University Extension: http://www.ext.colostate.edu/pubs/natres/06501.html

"*Crotalus viridis*: Western Rattlesnake." Valle, Laura. University of Michigan Museum of Zoology. Animal Diversity Web: http://animaldiversity.ummz.umich.edu/site/accounts/information/Crotalus_viridis.html

"Eastern Massasauga Rattlesnake: Why Conserve a Venomous Snake?" Endangered Species, Midwest Region, November 1999. U.S. Fish & Wildlife Service: http://www.fws.gov/midwest/endangered/reptiles/conserve.html

"Fast Facts: Prairie Rattlesnake." Animal Facts, Kids. Canadian Geographic: http://www. canadiangeographic.ca/kids/animal-facts/prairie_rattlesnake.asp

"List of Standard English and Current Scientific Names: Amphibians and Reptiles of New Mexico." Painter, Charles W. and James N. Stuart. University of New Mexico, Division of Amphibians & Reptiles, March 2004. Museum of Southwestern Biology: http://www.msb.unm.edu/herpetology/.../NM_species.htm

"Massasauga Rattlesnake." Dutton, Ian. Reptiles & Amphibians, October 2010. Suite101: http://www.suite101. com/content/massasauga-rattlesnake-a292700

"Modern Checklist of the Amphibians, Reptiles, and Turtles of Utah, A." Shofner, Ryan M. *Journal of Kansas Herpetology*, No. 21, March 2007. The Center for North American Herpetology: http://www.cnah.org/pdf_ files/685.pdf

"*Sistrurus catenatus tergeminus*: Western Massasauga." Snakebook. National Natural Toxins Research Center: http://ntrc.tamuk.edu/specieshtm/sctergeminus.htm

"Venomous Snakes of Colorado." P.R.E.S.E.R.V.E.: http://www.preservevenomous.com/Venomous_Snakes_ of_the_United_States/Venomous%20Snakes%20of%20Colorado/Venomous_snakes_of_Colorado.htm

Poole, Robert W. R. Nearctica.com, Inc.: http://www.nearctica.com/herps/snakes/viper/Cvirid.htm

Poole, Robert W. R. Nearctica.com, Inc.: http://www.nearctica.com/herps/snakes/viper/Scaten.htm

SKUNKS

"Skunk (Mepitidae)." Lamb, Annette and Larry Johnson. Living Things, May 2002. Eduscapes: http:// eduscapes.com/nature/skunk/index1.htm

"Skunks." Wildlife Species. Colorado Division of Wildlife: http://wildlife.state.co.us/WildlifeSpecies/ Profiles/Mammals/Skunk.htm

TURTLES

"Reptile Description: *Chelydra serpentina*, Snapping Turtle." Northern Rockies Natural History Guide. The University of Montana – Missoula: http://nhguide.dbs.umt.edu/index.php?c=reptiles&m=desc&id=12

"Spiny Softshell - *Apalone spinifera*." Montana Field Guide. Montana's Official State Website: http://fieldguide. mt.gov/detail_ARAAG01030.aspx

"Spiny Softshell: *Apalone spinifera*." State of Utah Natural Resources, Division of Wildlife Resources. Utah DNR: http://dwrcdc.nr.utah.gov/rsgis2/Search/Display.asp?FlNm=apalspin

RACCOONS

"*Baylisascaris procyonis*: An Emerging Helminthic Zoonosis." Sorvillo, Frank, Lawrence R. Ash, O. G. W. Berlin, JoAnne Yatabe, Chris Degiorgio and Stephen A. Morse. Emerging Infectious Diseases, *EID Journal*, Vol. 8, No. 4, April 2002. Centers for Disease Control and Prevention: http://wwwnc.cdc.gov/eid/article/8/4/01-0273_article.htm

COLLARED PECCARIES OR JAVELINAS

Arizona Game and Fish Department: http://www.azgfd.gov/

DesertUSA: http://www.desertusa.com/

"Javelina (or Peccary) (*Tayassu tajacu*)." Saguaro Juniper Corporation: http://www.saguaro-juniper.com/i_and_i/mammals/javelina/javelina.html

"Learn About Javelina." Ellisor, J. E. *Texas Parks & Wildlife Magazine*, June 1974. Texas Parks & Wildlife: http://www.tpwd.state.tx.us/publications/pwdpubs/media/pwd_lf_w7000_0146.pdf

"Living with Javelina, Myths and My Experience." Jones, Mike. ActiveRain Corp.: http://activerain.com/blogsview/1685198/living-with-javelina-myths-and-my-experience

"*Pecari tajacu*: Javelina." McCoy-Berney, Diane. Friends of Pinnacle Peak Park Newsletter, Fall 2006. Friends of Pinnacle Peak Park: http://www.pinnaclepeakpark.com/newsletter_fall_06.pdf

"Seed Predation and Dispersal by Peccaries throughout the Neotropics and its Consequences: a Review and Synthesis." Beck, Harald. Department of Biology, University of Miami, Coral Gables, 2004. Academia: http://towson.academia.edu/HaraldBeck/Papers/38569/Seed_predation_and_dispersal_by_peccaries_throughout_the_Neotropics_and_its_consequences_a_review_and_synthesis

Smithsonian National Zoological Park: http://nationalzoo.si.edu/

COYOTES

"Coyote Management: A Rationale For Population Reduction." Wade, Dale A. DigitalCommons@University of Nebraska - Lincoln, Wildlife Damage Management, Internet Center for Great Plains Wildlife Damage Control Workshop Proceedings, October 1981. University of Nebraska, Lincoln: http://digitalcommons.unl.edu/cgi/viewcontent.cgi?article=1146&context=gpwdcwp

"Coyote Threat Reaches 'Fever Pitch': DOW Reports 'Tsunami' of Calls." Denver News, February 2009. ABC 7 News: http://www.thedenverchannel.com/news/18693976/detail.html

Hatler, David F., David W. Nagorsen and Alison M. Beal. *Carnivores of British Columbia: Royal BC Museum Handbook*. Royal British Columbia Museum, 2008.

"Take Action! Urge Greenwood Village (CO) to Adopt an Ecologically and Ethically Sound Coyote Management Plan." Action Alert, May 2009. Project Coyote: http://www.projectcoyote.org/newsreleases/news_greenwood.html

GILA MONSTERS

Arizona Herpetological Association: http://www.azreptiles.com/

Arizona Poison & Drug Information Center. Phone: 1.800.222.1222. College of Pharmacy. The University of Arizona: http://www.pharmacy.arizona.edu/centers/arizona-poison-drug-information-center

Brown, David E. and Neil B. Carmony. *Gila Monster: Facts and Folklore of America's Aztec Lizard*. University of Utah Press, 2010.

DocSeward: http://www.docseward.com/

"Gila Monster." Fact Sheets. Smithsonian National Zoological Park: http://nationalzoo.si.edu/Animals/ReptilesAmphibians/Facts/FactSheets/Gilamonster.cfm

"Gila Monster (*Heloderma suspectum*)." Arizona-Sonora Desert Museum: http://www.desertmuseum.org/books/nhsd_gila.php'

"Gila Monsters in Our Midst: Living With an Ancient Native of St. George." Beck, Daniel. Division of State Parks & Recreation. State of Utah Natural Resources: http://wildlife.utah.gov/pdf/gila_monster_brochure.pdf

Hare, Trevor. *Poisonous Dwellers of the Desert: Description, Habitat, Prevention, Treatment*. Southwest Parks and Monuments Association, 1995.

Lowe, Charles H., Cecil R. Schwalbe and Terry B. Johnson. *The Venomous Reptiles of Arizona*. Arizona Game and Fish Department, 1986.

Tvedten, Steve. Non-Toxic Pest Control. Get Set, Inc.: http://www.getipm.com/

COUGARS

Busch, Robert H. *The Cougar Almanac: A Complete Natural History of the Mountain Lion*. The Lyons Press, 2004.

"Car Accident Statistics." Car-Accidents: http://www.car-accidents.com/pages/stats.html

"Claws." Cat Behavior. Animal Planet: http://animal.discovery.com/cat-guide/cat-anatomy/cat-claws.html

"Cougars on the Move." Kemper, Steve. *Smithsonian Magazine*, September 2006. Science & Nature, Smithsonian: http://www.smithsonianmag.com/science-nature/cougars.html

Hatler, David F., David W. Nagorsen and Alison M. Beal. *Carnivores of British Columbia: Royal BC Museum Handbook*. Royal British Columbia Museum, 2008.

Smith, Dave. *Don't Get Eaten: The Dangers of Animals that Charge or Attack*. Mountaineers Books, 2003.

BEARS

Anderson, Tom. *Black Bear: Seasons in the Wild*. Voyageur Press, 1992.

"Bear Spray vs. Bullets: Which Offers Better Protection?" Living with Grizzlies, Fact Sheet No. 8, Mountain-Prairie Region. U.S. Fish & Wildlife Service: http://www.fws.gov/mountain-prairie/species/mammals/grizzly/bear%20spray.pdf

Gookin, John and Tom Reed. *NOLS Bear Essentials: Hiking and Camping in Bear Country*. Stackpole Books, 2009.

Hatler, David F., David W. Nagorsen and Alison M. Beal. *Carnivores of British Columbia: Royal BC Museum Handbook*. Royal British Columbia Museum, 2008.

Herrero, Stephen. *Bear Attacks: Their Causes and Avoidance*. The Lyons Press, 1985.

Smith, Dave. *Don't Get Eaten: The Dangers of Animals that Charge or Attack*. Mountaineers Books, 2003.

RABIES

"Rabies." Centers for Disease Control and Prevention: http://www.cdc.gov/rabies/

"Rabies." Colorado Department of Public Health and Environment, Disease Control and Environmental Epidemiology Division. Colorado, The Official State Web Portal: http://www.cdphe.state.co.us/dc/zoonosis/rabies/index.html

"Rabies." Infectious Diseases. Eastern Idaho Public Health District: http://www.phd7.idaho.gov/Infectious%20Disease/Rabies/rabiesmain.html

"Rabies." Montana Fish, Wildlife & Parks. Montana's Official State Website: http://fwp.mt.gov/wildthings/livingWithWildlife/bats/bats_rabies.html

"Rabies: General Information." World Health Organization: http://www.who.int/rabies/epidemiology/Rabiessurveillance.pdf

"Rabies in Wyoming." Preventive Health and Safety Division. Wyoming Department of Health: http://www.health.wyo.gov/phsd/epiid/rabies.html

"Recent Evidence of Rabies in Montana Bats, Officials Warn." Department of Public Health & Human Services, July 2005. Montana's Official State Website: http://www.dphhs.mt.gov/newsevents/newsreleases2005/july/recentevidence.shtml

"To Help Deer—Don't Feed Them: Feeding Can Do More Harm Than Good." Wildlife Species. Colorado Division of Wildlife: http://wildlife.state.co.us/WildlifeSpecies/LivingWithWildlife/Mammals/

Photo credits by photographer and page number

Gary D. Alpert: 58

Scott Bauer/USDA Agricultural Research Service: 26

Rick and Nora Bowers/www.BowersPhoto.com: 105 (western spotted)

J.F. Butler: 50

Kim A. Cabrera: 108

David Cappaert: 55 (paper wasp)

Mark Cassino: 51

CDC/James Gathany: 23 (all)

Dan Downing: 27

Jerry W. Dragoo: 107

Dudley Edmondson: 99 (garter, hognose)

Dr. Dennis Feely/University of Nebraska Medical Center: 25, 28 (electron microscope images of deer tick)

Brad Fiero: 73 (striped-tail scorpion)

Tony Gallucci: 105 (hog-nosed)

Luther C. Goldman/USFWS: 93

Christine Hass: 105 (hooded)

Anthony Lau: 95

Tom Murray: 49 (both)

Gary Nafis: 85 (Hopi, Grand Canyon, Arizona black), 99 (gopher)

Lee Ostrom: 46 (hobo)

Jerry A. Payne/USDA Agricultural Research Service, Bugwood.org: 55 (yellow jacket)

Phil Pellitteri: 57 (underground nest)

Michael J. Plagens/www.arizonensis.org: 73 (bark scorpion)

Corey Raimond: 114

Stan Tekiela: 100, 106, 113 (spiny softshell, snapping)

About the Author

Tom Anderson is a professional naturalist, an award-winning writer and a wildlife expert. For 16 years he was director of the Lee and Rose Warner Nature Center, which is associated with the Science Museum of Minnesota and is located in Marine on St. Croix, Minnesota.

In addition to his work at the nature center, Tom is a well-known writer and columnist. For nearly 15 years he wrote "Reading Sign," an award-winning column for the *Chisago County Press*. He is also the author of 2 books, *Learning Nature by a Country Road* and *Black Bear: Seasons in the Wild*, both from Voyageur Press. He is a published poet and was a columnist for *Midwest Fly Fishing Magazine* and the Science Museum of Minnesota periodical, *Encounters*.

Tom has been honored many times for his writing. He was 1 of 20 Minnesota artists chosen to participate in the Millennium Journal Project. In 2003 he was awarded the "Best Commentary Award" by The National Association of Interpretation's periodical, *The Legacy*. In 2004 he was runner-up for the "Best Feature" category.

The natural world and our intimate connection to it inspires Tom to write. He lives southwest of North Branch, but he travels often, especially in the far North. He lives with his lovely wife, Nancy Conger, in the nineteenth-century farmhouse that his Swedish great-great grandparents built.

Tom's website is www.aligningwithnature.com.